POWER
IN YOUR
POCKET

Detox from Good Girl Syndrome

*and **rebel** from a life of 'shoulds'*

Jeanette Mundy and Laura Le Lievre

POWER IN YOUR POCKET:
Detox from Good Girl Syndrome

First published in Australia in 2020
By Heartnest
myheartnest@gmail.com

Copyright © 2020 by Jeanette Mundy and Laura Le Lievre.

Jeanette Mundy and Laura Le Lievre have asserted their rights under the Copyright, Designs and Patents Act 1988 to be identified as the authors of this work. The information in this book is based on the authors' experience and opinions. The publisher specifically disclaims responsibility for and adverse consequences, which may result from use of the information contained herein.

All rights reserved. No part of this publication may be reproduced, stored or transmitted in any form or by any means – whether auditory, graphic, scanning, mechanical or electronic – without written permission by the authors, except in the case of brief excerpts used in articles. Unauthorised reproduction of any part of this work is an illegal infringement of copyright.

National Library of Australia Cataloguing-inPublication entry:
Creators: Jeanette Mundy and Laura Le Lievre
ISBN
Print: 987 0 6487490 1 1
Ebook: 978 0 6487490 0 4

Edited by Linnet Hunter and Jeanette McLean
Cover design by Laura Le Lievre and Samuel Okike
Layout and typesetting by Samuel Okike

Photo credits: Laura Le Lievre, Nikki Olivier from NikkiOlivier.com plus the following photographers from Unsplash – Anita Austvika, David Veksler, Jez Timms, Michelle Dind, Nathan Dumlao, Paige Cody, Randy Fath, Rochelle Brown, Rodin Kutsaev, Rux Centea, Sai Kiran, Thomas Lefebre and Yang Shuo.

Publishing assistance by Publicious Book Publishing Services
www.publicious.com.au

Preface

HISTORY OF WOMEN'S POCKETS

Over 100 years ago, there were typically no pockets manufactured in women's clothing.

At this time there were women who hand-sewed large pockets into their dresses. They left their expected place of work – their kitchens. After loading up those pockets with pamphlets, they hit the streets to campaign for the right to vote. The pamphlets represented the power they had – their voices. They refused to be Good Girls because they knew that to bring about change meant to go against the status quo. These women became known as the Suffragettes.

Throughout history, countless women of all nationalities have also stood up against inequality and the expectations placed on them because of their gender. They have paved the way for each of us to stand up, have a voice and pursue whatever we want to.

Join the rising movement that's challenging the outdated beliefs that women are less-than just by being **you** and exercising the power that is within you.

Acknowledgements

Firstly, we want to express our gratitude for the courageous women who have inspired us and shared with us their barriers, struggles and successes. It's been an honour to see them reclaim their own authority. Without them, this book would not have been birthed.

We are in deep gratitude to NEIS (New Enterprise Incentive Scheme) at Holmesglen, Melbourne, to Michael La Scaleia and the fantastic teachers. Thank you too to NEIS business mentors Chelsea Hollins and Brett Stavenuiter for your invaluable help and strong belief in getting this message out to the world.

Thank you to Helen Heaney, Eve Wintergreen, Shelley Wade and Meridith Berrington for taking the time to provide valuable, imperative feedback and for your input in the manuscript process. You have all helped us dig deeper and persist at refining the book for its powerful messaging.

Thank you to our dedicated editing team – Linnet Hunter and Jeanette McLean. Linnet, we are so thankful for your expertise as a Creative Communications Coach (at www.wildsky.coach). We are in deep gratitude for your laser-sharp expertise in the use of language. Your input and belief in our message has helped us to communicate it in the most powerful way. Jeanette, we are in deep gratitude for your encouragement, dedication and constant support. The generous gift of your time and your owl-like eyes in piecing parts of the manuscript together for optimum clarity – and sharpening our sentences throughout the process – has enabled us to make the book what it is today.

Thank you to Jane Turner from Write with Jane. You championed us and gave us the opportunity to speak at your Authors Showcase at the NSW State Library and recommended us to speak at a Woman Economic Forum. We appreciate your expertise, advice and belief in us as authors.

Jeanette

Thank you to my dear friend and co-author Laura. You're living proof of a strong and courageous woman with the tenacity and drive to make a difference in the world. Traits that mirror my own makes us sisters on this path and I'm forever grateful for your creativity and skillful writing and organising of words to make sense.

I would like to thank my husband David for your patience, encouragement and growing belief in my message. For your understanding and conviction that there is no place in the world for abuse and disrespect. For your unconditional love and presence in the lives of our three girls and grandchildren. To my three incredible daughters, Lisa, Tali and Rachel for your belief in me. You drive me to make an impact every single day. You're all amazing, strong and courageous women whose daily practice of equality, standing up for what you believe in and living your dreams inspires me. Thank you for bringing laughter and joy to my world.

To my three incredible grandchildren, Charlotte, Audrey and Oscar (and any future grandchildren). You give me a bigger **why** for creating a world where inequality is eradicated. Your funny, quirky little ways remind me to see the world through the curiosity of a child.

To my sisters, Margo, Debbie, Helen and Sandy for your love and belief in me. Thanks for the times you've opened up to me about your own memories and perspectives of our childhood together. A special mention to my sister Helen. You are one of my biggest cheerleaders. Your belief in me inspires me to keep going. Our rich conversations always seem to expand my worldview and challenge me to think outside the ever persistent biases surrounding all of us. Quite honestly, I wouldn't be the person I am now without you.

I thank my wonderful ontological family, who are mentors and dear friends – Alan Sieler of Newfield Institute, Tony Carew of Liberated Leaders and Linnet Hunter from WildSky. Each one of you has supported me and helped me grow in ways you could not imagine. You have been the bedrock for my continued growth, self-belief and courage.

Finally, I am grateful to my dad for giving me the gift of ambition and the skills to lead a room full of people. Thank you to my mum for the gift of resilience, accepting me unconditionally, and for never ever judging me. Long after you are gone, your warm heart echoes the reassuring comment *don't worry about it* every time I'm faced with life's challenges.

Laura

To my beautiful friend and co-author Jeanette… you compliment my creativity with your own, and never ceases to inspire me with your ontological knowledge. I've loved all the laughing and learning we have had together in our writing and entrepreneurship journey.

I'd would like to thank my three daughters – my three J's – for giving me the biggest **why** for sharing a powerful message. Your resilience through challenging circumstances, resourcefulness and love of creativity never fails to inspire me. Your strong belief in equality – that girls, boys, men and women can achieve whatever they want to and make a difference in the world, fired my passion for this book. To my younger two J's: thank you for your delicious cups of tea – they hugely helped the words to flow!

I'm in deep gratitude for my Auntie J through the years. Thank you for your unwavering belief in me being destined for big things. I'm also thankful for your support, sunshine-like positivity, laughs, your faith and prayers – and to my Uncle Ross for your support in the quiet, but oh-so-important background. You both helped me have wings… and in turn, that has flowed to my girls too.

I'd like to thank my dear friends for making sure I practice the self-care I preach.

Thank you to Hayley, Andy and Mila for welcoming my girls to play while I tapped away at the keyboard. Knowing my girls were so happy enabled me to keep delving into the book. June and Ian Steward: I'm so grateful for your friendship and for launching me into the world as a writer and copywriter – I can't thank you enough.

To Jan and Gary McMahon and family: thank you for having me in your family, and making me give myself self-care in my late teens and beyond when I needed it most.

Thank you to my Dad Douglas and Mum Erica for giving Neil and I the paddocks to run wild on – it was the ultimate playground to explore, take risks and have adventures… and for showing me that both girls and boys can ride motorbikes, milk cows, fix cars and wrestle Poll Dorset sheep – and whatever they set their minds to.

Thank you to Mum and Dad for showing me that both girls and boys can ride motorbikes, milk cows, fix cars and wrestle poll dorset sheep – and whatever they set their minds to.

Thank you to my Mum for the way your face lit up when you saw me. You always made me feel valued, special, heard and loved. I'll never forget your warm kindness for humanity, patience, hugs and fresh-baked biscuits. You are in my heart every single day. Thank you for showing me that with strength, tenacity, resourcefulness and creativity, girls and women can be without limits.

And finally, thank you to my Creator for that small but powerful inner voice – inner gut – leading me. I've been shown over and over that we never need to be alone… and that standing strong as women is our right and our destiny.

Contents

Preface iii
    HISTORY OF WOMEN'S POCKETS iii

Acknowledgements v

A Note From the Authors xi

Introduction xv
    A CULTURE OF CHANGE xv

Chapter 1: Epidemic Inequality 1
    TIME FOR CHANGE 1

Chapter 2: Your Story 15
    FACING THE SHADOWS 15

Chapter 3: Pull the Plug on People Pleasing 27
    STEP INTO YOUR OWN AUTHORITY 27

Chapter 4: Being Enough 39
    DITCHING PERFECTION IN A WORLD OF EXPECTATION . 39

Chapter 5: Ditch Comparisons 49
    EMBRACE YOUR UNIQUENESS 49

Chapter 6: Delete Should 57
    NO MORE RULES 57

Chapter 7: Emotions 65
    YOUR INNER GUIDE 65

Chapter 8: Overwhelm and Burnout **79**
    FIND YOUR INNER CALM... 79

Chapter 9: Listen To Your Gut.................................**97**
    WHEN THINGS DON'T FEEL RIGHT..97

Chapter 10: The Power of Your Words **103**
    FINDING YOUR VOICE.. 103

Chapter 11: Set Clear Boundaries **115**
    FREEDOM FROM CONTROL.. 115

Chapter 12: Spring-Clean Your Friends List.......... **129**
    CHOOSE YOUR CHEERLEADERS.. 129

Chapter 13: Coming home **139**
    WHERE RESPECT AND EQUALITY IS CULTIVATED............. 139

Chapter 14: Put Yourself First **147**
    SELF-CARE THAT FOSTERS YOUR GROWTH........................... 147

Chapter 15: Reflecting Forward **157**
    A VISION FOR THE FUTURE 157

About the Authors.. **161**

Reference List **165**

A Note From the Authors

Jeanette

Have you had a moment when someone told you that you didn't measure up?

My father was very surprised when at the age of 75 he learned that a woman could actually be the director of her own company. In that moment I felt compelled to be the cheerleader of women – and of me.

Yes! Women can do anything you know dad! I retorted.

Before I got a chance to remind him I was actually the director of my own business, he swifty replied: *Oh, don't you put yourself in that category Jeanette!*

His attempt to knock me down echoed in my thoughts long enough to remember why it's so important to share this message. So that women can believe in themselves in spite of being told they are not enough.

At an earlier time, as I walked across the road to school, dad yelled at me, *Get off the road you stupid bloody idiot!*

Highly embarrassed and ashamed, I collapsed into my body and tried to stay as invisible as possible. This was my body's wonderful way of protecting me. What I didn't realise at the time was that the strong and powerful words of criticism were imprinted into my emotional memory.

If this had been one isolated event, backed up with love and approval, I don't believe it would have affected me quite as much as it did. But it wasn't an isolated event. Approval never came from the person I was seeking it from the most.

As I grew up feeling invisible and nervous to put a foot wrong. I also learned (wrongly) that men are the authority and women are submissive and unworthy.

I made constant attempts to show people I was worthy. Deep down though, I was trying to prove it to myself. I was smart yet my earlier experiences had me believing I was stupid. I found it hard to learn so I skipped as much school as I could get away with and finished with a fail at the end of year ten. I wanted to go back and repeat but I was offered an easier road. As a female teenager in the 70's I didn't see the possibilities in front of me so I took it. The way I was modeled what a woman should be and could be, shaped my belief about what I believed was possible for me. My experiences have shaped me, and have given me the gift of learning.

I'm no longer resentful and angry about my experience. In fact, I feel compassion, love and empathy toward both my parents.

Through my experience I didn't feel like I had a right to have a voice. It led me to seek external validation and to find purpose and meaning through that validation. I continually supported others and found ways to be noticed. In doing so I found myself being everything to everyone else and playing small. I became anxious and I hated the thought of someone giving me even a little bit of negative feedback, because negative feedback confirmed to me that I was 'stupid'. This was all the catalyst for self-doubt.

The cost – I never showed up for myself. The result? **Good Girl Syndrome!**

My experiences led me to study Ontological Coaching, and through that incredible training I've developed more confidence, resilience, strength and unapologetic drive. These qualities have helped me to embrace my fragility and push on with courage and determination.

Laura

Have you ever felt the weight of expectations on you... to later realise you had carried that weight simply because you were female?

I was 15-years-old when I remember holding a weight like this.

I was standing at the top of the driveway with my father and brother. It was the day of my beautiful Mum's funeral. In the afternoon, relatives had said goodbye. I watched as each of their cars disappeared down the hill with a sinking and empty feeling in my gut. They had their families and lives to go back to – I understood that completely. At the same time, I wasn't sure how I would cope without my beautiful mum, who was never coming back.

That was the moment I began to truly realise what role in my family I felt I must now play. In my mind I thought: *Oh, my gosh. I have a big job to do – and how am I going to do it?* It was clear to me that as the female left in the house, I was now to be the homemaker. I loved my family and believed that was how I was supposed to show them I loved them. I subconsciously believed my worth in my family was dependent on me fulfilling this role to a high standard in my mum's place. It made me grow up quickly... and had me in the pattern of putting others first.

Years later, I automatically took on this role in my marriage. Under respectful circumstances this may have worked. However, the environment became disrespectful, unpredictable... and abusive. This was the beginning of losing myself in the attempt of taming an out-of-control fire... and times of a confusing or high-conflict environment. Finally realising after close to nine years of marriage that I couldn't do or say anything that would ever ensure a home of consistent respect and safety, I escaped with my girls in tow.

It was a shock to learn how common this is for women, children – and some men too. And it shouldn't be. How are our children going to know what healthy, respectful relationships are? They absorb how they and others around them are treated... and their reality becomes their ongoing normal.

My experience has led me on a journey where I had the space to rediscover myself again and create a home for my girls where they could do the same. By facing the past, undoing the conditioning to be over-responsible for others and challenging myself one small step at a time, I've become more of the person I feel I was always meant to be. Even better, I love the fact that this process of growth never needs to stop for any of us.

Introduction

A CULTURE OF CHANGE

Many women around the globe are coming to the realisation that they've put themselves last for most of their lives.

> *Throughout centuries, from the moment a baby girl is born, she is assigned a role...*

She quickly learns what is expected of her as a Good Girl. She is praised for being pretty, accommodating and nice. The repeated approval of what it means to be good conditions her to put herself last... hello Good Girl Syndrome.

Absorbing the unequal traditions and attitudes around her, she repeatedly hears what girls and women should and shouldn't do. She sees the media objectify women. And she sees the roles men and women play – at home, in public and on TV. All this shapes her as she grows up. It shapes how she sees the world and how she sees her place in it. It's her normal, it's what she knows. It just **is**.

She is talked over and dismissed when her ideas are perceived as stepping on toes. She keeps the peace when she is put in her place for being bossy. She doesn't always have the confidence to ask for what she wants in the way that she really wants it, and often, she jumps in to say yes before she thinks about the promise she's making.

She grows up... and so do her expectations on herself. If she partners, she goes through an adjustment and a recalibration of her life. If children come into the picture, family and work life become a constant juggle. She often finds herself being the go-to person, the one who remembers all the little things like water bottles, buying more socks, dental checkups and what's for tea. It's when she mistakenly thinks she is entirely responsible for the happiness of everyone else that she is sacrificing her own happiness. The mental load she carries weighs her down. She is overwhelmed, exhausted and disillusioned. After all, Good Girl conditioning says, *You have to be everything to everyone else, because you are meant to be the nurturer, supporter and organiser.* This conditioning has left us feeling not enough if we don't.

But it doesn't have to stay that way. Many women just like her are coming to the conclusion that the old social narrative of being everything to everyone else isn't sustainable. If she doesn't want to be a part of that old story, she doesn't have to be.

The flow-on from inequality has meant that many women have danced on eggshells. But more and more of us are stamping on them.

We are putting more energy into ourselves. The Information Age has given us **knowledge is power.** We can type anything into a search engine and find the answers to our questions. Through fast modes of transport and the world wide web, we are all connected like never before.

Women are beginning to step outside old paradigms such as Good Girl, learning new things and deciding how they want to spend their time. They are sharing **their** gifts with the world, rather than taking a back seat and playing a supporting role to other people's freedom at the expense of their own.

We don't have to put ourselves last any longer – and to do so would be sad for all humanity. Women have so much to give and immeasurable talents and innovative ideas to share with the world without sacrificing themselves for the greater good.

Detoxing from Good Girl Syndrome means changing the story of being everything to everyone – and finding ways to put ourselves first. It means honouring our intuition and following it. It means not asking for permission or seeking approval, but giving it to ourselves. It means doing what we want.

We have choices about the types of conversations we have, the things we listen to, and the things we take on. To be our own authority, it means making clear requests so that we're not always taking on everyone else's responsibilities and sacrificing our own time. It's about getting really clear about what we do want to take on – and how well these responsibilities will serve us for what we want to create in the world.

Detoxing from Good Girl Syndrome means doing courageous things even when we are scared. It means exploring our interests, expressing our thoughts and sharing our gifts and creativity. It means doing what really matters to us.

It means spending time nurturing our souls. We can't change the past, but we can use the wisdom we have gained to sharpen our inner guide – our intuition – into powerful actions to create the future we want. We have the power within us to write a brand new, exciting narrative.

This also means when someone around us is uncomfortable with how they see us grow and change, we can accept it and continue to stand strong and in doing so, disrupt the status quo. When we do that for ourselves, it creates a ripple effect of courage and ambition for other women, girls and boys too.

We trust this book will help you get back to **you** and inspire even more possibilities for a bright future you can get excited about. We hope that through this book you continue to become your own trusted inner guide – with extra power in your pocket.

– Laura and Jeanette

How to use this book

As we move through the phases of our lives we change, but many of us still look back over our lives with regret that we haven't fulfilled our hopes and dreams.

As you read through this book, we invite you to consider the way Good Girl conditioning may have prevented you for asking for what you want, sharing your wisdom and living your dreams.

We believe that's possible when each of us are observers of our current situation through a different lens – and observe how our environment and experiences play a part in shaping our past and current choices.

While the order of the chapters is designed to take you on a journey, feel free to pick out and read any one chapter at a time that stands out to you.

At the end of each chapter we've also included key points you can come back to at any time. You'll also find Power Actions which are designed so you can take action right away. These actions will help you move from reading, to knowing, to becoming. Each action will help you undo Good Girl Syndrome conditioning, one small but powerful step at a time.

Chapter 1

Epidemic Inequality

TIME FOR CHANGE

If you've grown up with very little inequality, you're one of the fortunate few. However, the reality is that it's all around us, whether or not we can see it clearly. Society has been built on gender stereotyping and inequality, and most of us have adapted our living around that.

This becomes our normal and it blends into our everyday living. This is why we don't see it. From the time we were little girls we were like sponges, soaking in the messages that conditioned us to play our gender roles.

In her TED Talk, 'Seven Beliefs that Can Silence Women – And How to Unlearn Them', Deepa Narayan speaks about what makes Good Girls. She talks about seven beliefs that are considered good and moral that women have taken on since they were girls, such as always pleasing others before themselves. She says, *Everyone likes a nice woman who always smiles, who never says no, is never angry even when she's being exploited.*

She goes on to say:

All these seven habits that we thought were good and moral snatch life away from girls and position men to abuse. We must change. How do we change? A habit is just a habit. Every habit is a learned habit. So we can unlearn them. And this personal change is extremely important. I had to change too.

Deepa explains how girls in India and around the world are conditioned to give up their dreams. She says, *Such girls give up their dreams, their desires... and nobody even notices. Except for depression. It moves in.*

Have you noticed the sexual objectification of girls and women, particularly when they reach puberty? As adults we can be leaders in this space and awaken to how gender inequality and sexualisation of girls and women has affected us personally.

Facing up to what's out there and making our girls resilient and strong isn't going to be easy. You may also have to look at yourself to see whether the creeping sexualisation of society has affected your values too. But if this helps your daughter be a little more true to herself, rather than feeling she has to fit into today's stifling stereotypes of good looks and 'sexiness', we will have won back some of her freedom to live without these constraints. If we don't succeed, the price is high for our girls.

– Tanith Carey, *Where Has My Little Girl Gone?*

It's time for change. We first need to face these messages that have created these unequal beliefs. It's when we truly see them and know we have the right to challenge them, that we can change the habits and roles we have been conditioned to believe we must play. Then we can set ourselves free from every limitation they impose upon us and find new ways of being in the world without them.

So how does it begin?

At home... and in the playground

Attitudes of inequality have been embedded within our culture, from generation to generation through history... at home, in the playground and beyond.

In her e-book *How to Raise Confident Girls,* Elena Favilli speaks about why empowering girls is so hard – and why it matters. She links how boys and girls are raised with the gender biases and gender expectations placed on them in adulthood.

Elena says, *Take cooking for example. Today women in general are more likely to do housework than men. But why is that? Is it because women are born* with a cooking gene or is it because over the years they have been taught over and over to see cooking as their role?

... it's the culture that we make that exaggerate these differences and then turns them into a self-fulfilling prophecy. So if you're a girl, you're supposed to naturally like cooking and if you're a boy, you're supposed to naturally like sport, until someone points out that the majority of famous cooks in the world are men.

Has gender inequality been that bad for women?

Gender inequality affects every level of society and every nationality. In the suburbs, a woman and her two young children are being turned down on numerous housing applications... and in the halls of Parliament and in the offices of CEOs, women are more likely than not to play a supportive role.

The Equality Rights Alliance states that the problem is still a current one in Australia: *Gender inequality continues to be a major barrier to the realisation of rights and access to opportunities for girls and women in Australia.*

It was not long ago in Australia that women were so unequally treated that they were considered the property of their husbands. A husband could not be charged with rape or sexual assault as marriage was considered a contract for sex. Finally, in 1994, marital rape was criminalised in every state of Australia.

It wasn't until November 18, 1966 that all married women were permitted to work in Public Service in Australia.

The bar on employment of married women in the Commonwealth Public Service is abolished. Introduced at the beginning of the 1900s, the 'marriage bar' was intended to keep women from 'stealing' men's jobs and also to boost the birth rate. It meant many women kept their marriages a secret.

– Kathy Gollan, *ABC Earshot*, Marriage Bar Abolished, Marriage in Australia: A Timeline of How Love and Law Have Changed in 130 Years

The law has changed, but how many women and men have continued to live with the acute or subtle attitudes that have stemmed from what used to be accepted practice?

Inequality in high places

In the political arena we see men appointed to high profile roles and women being objectified. An assertive and skilled politician can very quickly be criticised for her physical appearance, her outfits and her life choices – and her intelligence questioned in a way we never see applied to a man.

During a Q&A session on the ABC with Julia Gillard, Hilary Clinton said, *The double standard is alive and well and it is more difficult for women in public positions – we'll talk about politics, but it's true in business, it's true in the media, it's just true across the board – because there are expectations about women's appearance that are deep in our collective DNA. So that people feel free to comment – either favourably or unfavourably about hair styles, clothing fashions and all the rest of it. Some of that is because we are still getting used to seeing women in these roles... In politics men come in all sizes and shapes, all kinds of hair styles, or no hair at all and it is not remarked upon, because you are used to seeing men in these roles...*

Hilary also mentioned a prominent political leader who attacked a women competitor: *He didn't attack her successful business background or her views on issues. He attacked her face.*

She went on to explain her belief as to why women leaders have their appearance criticised: *There is still a very large proportion of the population that is uneasy with women in positions of leadership. And so the easiest way to (kind of) avoid having to look at someone on her merits is to dismiss her on her looks...*

Hillary related this to the dislike she sees women face in politics: *The research is pretty clear. For men, likeability and professional success go hand-in-hand. In other words, the more successful a man becomes, the more people like him. But with women it's the exact opposite. The more professionally successful we are, the less people like us.*

She made further comments that people really like her personally when she's in a supporting role, but, *The minute that I, or any woman, stands up and says, 'now I'd like a chance to lead', that approval changes.*

Hilary also acknowledged that women didn't just encounter this inequality in politics, saying... *in those quiet places, at work, in the community, sometimes even in one's family, there are challenges.*

When we see it in the highest ranks of politics we are dished up a reality check that it may always be there, flowing down from the top – and trickling into organisations, businesses, councils and behind closed doors – in homes of everyday people just like us.

We can use opportunities to speak up against gender inequality and make a difference, and we can also lead by example. There's nothing more powerful to future generations than past generations deciding to step outside the status quo.

Inequality in the everyday workforce

Only 22% of all professionals globally are women, according to The Global Gender Gap Report, 2018.

On average, women spend twice as much time on unpaid work as men, as reported by the Australian Bureau of Statistics, 2016. Women also have about half as much money for their retirement, as evidenced in a Parliament of Australia Inquiry in 2016.

The Human Rights Commission highlighted that between 2011 and 2016 homelessness had increased for women over the age of 55 by 31%. Women earning less money across their lifetime than men was a significant contributor.

Sexism and inequality flows into other parts of women's lives too. Gender roles such as motherhood result in many women finding themselves pushed into a no-win corner.

For example, in many families inequality is still alive and thriving. If a woman has career goals and aspirations, she may cringe at the mere thought of attempting to fulfill them while juggling her invisible, gendered loads. Even if this does not seem like gender inequality to some people, a woman can find herself constantly fighting off the entitlement of others who vocalise their opinions regarding her life choices. One opinion may support the view that she should be a full-time stay-at-home mum. Another may support going back to work to reduce family financial pressure, while another supports the view that women have a right to and should be encouraged to fulfil their career aspirations. Many women experience guilt and confusion around these opinions.

> *The trick is to shape your own values, live by these and be comfortable with your choices.*

Unconscious bias both women and men face

In *Quarterly Essay: Men at Work*, Australian political journalist and podcaster Annabel Crabb expressed her anger that women in leadership were typically asked how they managed their work and family responsibilities. She expresses her anger on behalf of both men and women when she stated that men in leadership are **not** asked that question. Her argument? A father having an active role in his children's daily care should be equally valued and respected.

Annabel writes, *Now I just get mad when male leaders aren't asked it. Not asking is actually, in itself, quite a powerful message. It says, 'No one expects you to care about this.' It says, 'It's not your job to worry about that stuff.' It says, 'Whatever efforts you do make, or whatever private griefs your big job cloaks, are not of interest to anyone.' And for an increasing number of young fathers who do want to live their lives differently from the way their own fathers did, that's an insult.*

Perhaps we could ask ourselves if this indicates that it is still largely a woman's role to manage parental responsibilities – even in a world where both men and women are expected to be in the paid workforce. It is through conversations that light is shed on these unconscious biases.

> *Change is coming and we can be a part of that change by stepping into our own power and allowing ourselves to seek possible pathways for our careers and futures.*

The darker side of inequality

Inequality is a seed. When attitudes of inequality are watered with increasing disrespect, the weeds that grow from this can manifest into relationship mistreatment and abuse.

Kate Jenkins, Sex Discrimination Commissioner says, *Research in Australia has shown the primary reason some men feel entitled to treat women as lesser is because, as a whole, there is a view about the roles men and women should play.*

According to The Australian Bureau of Statistics 2017, one in three women have experienced violence since the age of fifteen (this is identical to the worldwide statistic mentioned further down).

When speaking about abuse primarily affecting women and children behind closed doors, Lundy Bancroft refers to inequality being at the root.

Entitlement is the abuser's belief that he has a status and that it provides him with exclusive rights and privileges that do not apply to his partner... Abuse grows from attitudes and values, not feelings. The roots are ownership, the trunk is entitlement, and the branches are control.

— Lundy Bancroft, *Why Does He Do That? In the Minds of Angry and Controlling Men*

Even when gender inequality morphs into abuse and mistreatment, to an untrained eye, these behaviours largely remain invisible.

I was like sweet, little Bambi, skipping joyfully through the forest, with so much innocence and trust. I didn't realise that in the shadows was a hungry wolf in sheep's clothing.

— Eve W.

In all societies, to varying degrees, women and girls are subjected to physical, sexual and psychological abuse that cuts across lines of income, class and culture. Such violence is recognised as a violation of human rights and a form of discrimination against women, reflecting the pervasive imbalance of power between women and men.

— United Nations, 2015

The World Health Organisation *(WHO)* states, *Global estimates indicate that about one in three women (35%) worldwide have experienced either physical and/or sexual intimate partner violence or non-partner sexual violence.*

Tarana Burke, original founder of the social media Me Too Movement, says that we can start building a world free of sexual abuse in particular by dismantling the building blocks of sexual violence: **power and privilege**. She also says, *We must recognise that any person sitting in a position of power comes with privilege, rendering those without power vulnerable.*

We reshape the imbalance of power by raising our voices against it in unison, by creating spaces that speak truth to power. We have to re-educate ourselves and our children to understand that power and privilege doesn't always have to destroy and take – it can be used to serve and build.

– Tarana Burke

Where had Tarana's inspiration come from? It had come from her experience back in 1997 of a 13-year-old girl confiding in Tarana that she had been sexually abused. When the girl walked away, Tarana was left without words.

I didn't have a response or a way to help her in that moment, and I couldn't even say 'me too', lamented Tarana. *It really bothered me, and it stayed in my spirit for a long time.*

Ten years later, Tarana supported survivors of sexual violence, initially for black women and girls from low socioeconomic communities and later for greater society. Her nonprofit organisation Just Be Inc. was created to connect survivors to resources and encouragement to empower them. She gave the movement a name – **Me Too**.

In 2019 the hashtag #metoo went viral when Alyssa Milano posted on Twitter in response to a high profile movie producer's alleged sexual abuse. She urged fellow women to also use the hashtag if they had also experienced sexual violence. The online world was taken over with millions of women using the hashtag #metoo. Their stories activated a wave of conversations about the trauma and sexism they'd experienced because they were female.

Shortly after, the Me Too Movement gained momentum. It continued to interrupt sexual abuse and gained more strength in the spotlight. And for Tarana it's **never** been about demonising men. It's about supporting every person who is a survivor of sexual violence: girls and boys, women, men, the transgender community, various ethnic and religious backgrounds, and women from indigenous communities. It's about encouraging conversations in homes, in communities, and workplaces to bring in inclusivity and respect.

We have to dramatically shift a culture that propagates the idea that vulnerability is synonymous with permission. It's a culture that says body autonomy is not a basic human right.

– Tarana Bourke, founder of the Me Too Movement

This movement is one example of inspiration for change. There are many other positive movements for change involving both men and women standing up against inequality and abuse. This is encouraging because even when we feel at our most vulnerable, we can remind ourselves that there is light shining on equal rights for all.

While we might feel vulnerable in a world where domestic violence and sexual objectification is so common, the more we step into our power, the more confident our actions will become.

While global change is not your sole responsibility, becoming a powerful observer of the way your past has affected you, particularly if abuse has been a part of it, means you can leave it in the past – where it belongs. Then you can lead yourself into a future where you can do what you want in spite of it.

Story – The boys at the pool

I stood on the side of the pool, gazing in shock and disbelief at two little boys, both victims of domestic violence. I felt sick to the stomach at this new realisation. I was only 16. They were both from different families, both subjected to physical violence. One had visible physical scars. The other had obvious emotional scars – and both no doubt had invisible scars to their souls.

This was the first time I had seen or even heard of domestic violence. Inequality I was familiar with, but I didn't make a link between the abuse and inequality until much later.

I had no idea people could hurt each other in that way. It was for the movies. Until that moment, I was blissfully naive. The world paints an eerily similar picture today. There is one difference. Most of us have some awareness of what goes on silently inside normal homes every day… even teenagers.

After I recovered from the initial shock and deep sadness for these two children, I scanned the outside world in my brain, trying to make sense of it. What I would come to learn and am still learning is that this isn't a local problem – and it didn't start with abuse. It started with inequality. The perceptions and attitudes of society that women and children are somehow inferior to men, leads many men to treating them as inferior, and perceptions don't change when the invisible mess is so deeply ingrained.

My immediate thought on that day was, This has to stop! These boys are likely to commit the same abuse when they grow up unless someone or society steps in to break the cycle.

— Jeanette

> *Our specific mandate is to prevent violence against women and their children, but promoting gender equality and respectful and non-violent relationships benefits the whole community, including men.*
>
> *— Our Watch, ourwatch.org.au*

Moving beyond inequality

Gender inequality has a negative impact for everyone. When a woman is mistreated, children are immediately impacted. Families lose out. Many men are losing out too. If they are stuck in the gender conditioning of always having to be a strong man, this commonly impacts their ability to understand and freely express their emotions. This impacts on their experience of meaningful connection and happiness (that's a book in itself).

Some women are coveting the power they see men have – and they are taking on an aggressive alpha role, equating patriarchal power as something they can personally embody. When they exercise it over their partners and children for power, control and domination, it can be just as destructive as any inequality and abuse from a man.

And yet courage doesn't have to equal aggression.

In the world today we're finding more and more ways to move beyond inequality and yet we still see so much of it and have such a long way to go.

> *The change that is needed will come when we believe change is possible. And then from that belief we can cultivate strength, ambition and hope. From these moods we can begin to see the possibilities and have the conversations that will bring about the change we want to see. Then with courage we can make change happen.*

Courage means taking action even though we are afraid. Although the Good Girl conditioning has left many of us feeling vulnerable, this does not mean we cannot face our greatest fears with courage and boldness. Courage is no longer doing things for others at our own expense. It's about standing up and saying: *we no longer stand for this old narrative*, regardless of the fallout. There will always be uncertainties in anything worth taking a risk.

This is what detoxing from Good Girl Syndrome is all about.

My voice is strong and imposing, and my legs are powerful enough to hold up its weight. I wake up every day assured of my right to not only participate in the world as an equal part of it, but to loudly reject the narrative that keeps trying to tell me to pipe down, fold in, shrivel up, simper, apologise and slink my way through life so as not to offend or upset anyone with the complicated, beautiful mess that is me. I have fought the odds to get here, empowered by the knowledge that every single woman who has come before me has fought her own battle in order to survive. We fight like girls. This is how we prevail. And this is why we're still standing.

— Clementine Ford, *Fight Like a Girl*

POWER ACTION

Inequality reflection:

Observe the conversations in the media, your community and your families. Consider what you do and don't like. When you think about how it has impacted you, go one step further and ask yourself how you would like things to be in your future? What changes would you like to see?

Start taking action on the changes you want to see for yourself.

Key Points

- Gender inequality affects almost every girl and woman worldwide
- Both women and men can treat others unequally
- Attitudes of inequality are the seeds that lead to disrespect, mistreatment, abuse
- Attitudes that fuel inequality are chiefly patriarchal with domination and control at the root
- Inequality is bad for everyone
- With courage, we can overcome inequality by detoxing from Good Girl Syndrome

Chapter 2

Your Story

FACING THE SHADOWS

> *If we can share our story with someone who responds with empathy and understanding, shame can't survive.*
> – Brene Brown, Daring Greatly

Storytelling is a practice that has been shared through generations for thousands of years. Our own story is our life narrative. Sharing our story helps us process our experiences, make sense of the world and our place in it.

We hear the stories of others in our conversations, books we read, the movies we watch and these days the social media we immerse ourselves in. As we listen we are influenced by cultural and social narratives within the stories. Some of these shock and upset us. By watching and listening we learn about different cultures and their traditions, social practices and attitudes. This is our **her-story** and **his-story**.

What we learn from and through each others' stories are different ways of perceiving and interpreting our experiences and the world around us. We can also decide what we want to take on and what stories we want to change.

Sharing your story is beneficial to both yourself and the world because this act connects you with others and inspires action to transform the way you give, love and live.

– womenforone.com

NOTE: Going through our past story can be triggering for some of us. It's the triggers that can help us to learn from it. Seek help if you find you're not coping and are finding it traumatising in any way. Again, going into your story is healthy when you learn from it and find a way for it to help empower your future.

Our lives are infused with story

What are some outdated stories of inequality that still exist today?

- That women are tied to the kitchen and men are tied to the lawn mower?
- That women must sit quietly at the back of the room and listen to the wisdom of men?
- That women do not know how to look after themselves without a man in their lives?
- That men can't sufficiently look after children?
- That men are stronger leaders than women?
- That men aren't able to express themselves or aren't as good with their words?
- These beliefs are ingrained in our everyday practices and yet we are seeing evidence to the contrary everywhere. Isn't it ironic that women are frequently deemed better at expressing themselves but yet men are more likely to be accepted into leadership roles? And that women are still deemed to be the better, more nurturing parent but many men are now successfully taking on the role as primary caregivers?

Gender, family and community narratives (stories)

Being a Good Girl is a gender narrative

It might not be a narrative we're comfortable with, although we cannot deny our lives are infused with it. We've learned how to be a Good Girl through our everyday conversations with our family and community.

It's generations of conversations that have shaped these narratives. The risk is that we take them on as though they are the truth. It's not surprising we would do that because we're conditioned from a very early age. This conditioning influences our values, standards, behaviours and social practices. In essence, these are already set for us and it's not until we move into adulthood that we begin to shape our own and in doing so, shift away from traditions.

Traditionally, in many families, boys play with cars and girls play with dolls. There's nothing wrong with a child showing a preference, but when boys are shamed for playing with dolls and girls are told they're tomboys for playing with cars and taking risks, we feed into the narratives of gender stereotyping.

How can it be positive when a boy's strength or a girl's appearance is the sole focus? When a boy's strength or a girl's appearance is the dominant focus, it draws us away from the inner qualities and strengths of each individual.

Gender Stereotyping in our books and movies

The University of Copenhagen, in the article Women are Beautiful, Men Rational, wrote...

*A robot read 3.5 million books to see how we describe men and women differently. Beautiful, sexy and gorgeous were used most often to describe women. While men were most frequently called brave, rational and righteous, negative verbs about the body cropped up five times more often for women. And overall, adjectives used for women focused on **appearance**. While for men, **behaviour*** *was key. The robot reader analyzed 11 billion words from books dating back to 1900. It discovered gender bias in both fiction and non-fiction texts.*

How many movies have we seen that involve an attractive woman being chased and desired like a prize to be won? And how many of these movies show the man – the hero – winning her over?

Relationships

How did I get here?

How many of us have woken up one day and had the realisation that our relationship was not as we thought it would be?

In the beginning of a relationship it's easy to miss the types of conversations where we share our values, our beliefs and our role expectations. Even if we do have these conversations we may be left feeling dissatisfied when promises and commitments are broken. Self-awareness doesn't guarantee that our requests to have our partner share the load – or for them to support us to fulfill our career aspirations – will be heard.

What promises did we listened to in the beginning that were never made?

Many women are arriving at middle-age dissatisfied and empty.

Story – Rashelle's emptiness

When Rashelle's children left home she was lost. She declared that she no purpose anymore and believed she was no longer needed. She felt empty. Even though she had the freedom she yearned for, once that freedom came she didn't know how to harness it. Confused about the future, she questioned her value and and regretted that her life didn't turn out quite as she had expected.

Rashelle's confidence is low. Having lived in self-doubt all her life, she is worried that her skills are outdated. She's been everything to her family and now that they've left, she's wondering what she's going to do with the rest of her life. She needs to find something to give herself the purpose she continues to yearn for.

If we get great satisfaction and joy from our traditional role, then our story stays the same – and that's okay. That's our choice.

But we have a right to rewrite our story and if we want to. Rather than remaining dissatisfied and living a life without meaning, many women are changing that story but they're doing so with resistance because the gender narratives are so deeply ingrained.

In writing about cultural narratives, Alan Sieler, author of *Coaching to the Human Soul*, commented that an unspoken core belief that many women are living out is: *Women must be everything to everyone else and in the meantime they must suffer, and if they show up as confident they disrupt the status quo.* His observations highlighted the many invisible narratives and subsequent roles we play.

> *Each of us carries around in our nervous system, our interpretation of what happened in the past, as well as how the world is, could be and should be. It is from that interpretation that the world shows up for us.*
>
> – Alan Sieler

Story – Women are much better at these things

My mum had taught me that both women and men could do anything they set their minds to. Yet, after her death, what I saw on reflection was a strong woman balancing the world on her shoulders. I saw that I had consequently assumed it was my role, as a female, to fill her many shoes after she passed away. But was it really?

By the time I was seventeen, I questioned and challenged inequality. Why should women be responsible for doing the majority of housework and cooking if they were also on their feet working all day?

My dad would say, *Women are much better at these things.*

I'd disagree, saying, *No, they're not. But if you really think that, maybe men just need more practice, Dad.* I'd also remind him that the most famous chefs were men. I put my foot down and required my brother to help out here and there plus cook a meal at least once a week.

In my story there were two conflicting narratives. My mum desperately tried to teach me that I could do anythingI put my mind to. However, what I saw was different. Was she trapped in the gender narrative that *women are much better at these things*? Consequently, I found myself in her former role.

If we're silently believing we have to take on these gender roles, where does that leave us in trying to fulfill our hopes and dreams? Therefore, the way we interpret our circumstances matters.

The world is changing, and in many cultures and communities we see people crossing the gender stereotype boundaries without question. In some western cultures we see girls and boys comfortably choosing to step outside the status quo and parents encouraging choice. We see women step up as family, community and world leaders, entrepreneurs, women's advocates and disruptors. We see some men choosing to be primary caregivers. This change is both disruptive and necessary.

However, there are some tightly held outdated attitudes and perceptions that are still at play in government, families and communities. The world still has a long way to go before our eyes open wide to the biases and prejudices we are continually living in.

One thing we can all do today to start breaking down these outdated traditional beliefs is to open up conversations. We can speak up when we're feeling vulnerable, challenge our own beliefs, the beliefs of our friends and the beliefs we grew up in. We can also step up with courage to do what our heart desires no matter what uncertainties we face and take heart that no matter what, we can change our story, and in doing so change our future!

> *Our stories can help us be aware of outdated attitudes and social practices. The more we become aware of them **in our stories**, the bigger chance we have of taking part in change – especially our own change.*
>
> – Jeanette

The Resignation Trap

Resignation feeds procrastination, diversion and distraction when we don't believe we can make a difference.

Resignation is a mood that leaves us with the feeling that we have no control over the outcome of something. Even if we could have control over the outcome, our belief is that no matter what we do, nothing will make a difference, so we give up trying.

Many women still find it hard to say anything but yes when someone asks them to do something. Living in the story of obligation prevents them from seeing that they have a choice to respond with no, to pause before responding, or take their own needs into consideration and make a counter offer.

Living in resignation means that somehow deep within us we believe there is no point in trying in the first place, or even if we did try, we are highly unlikely to get what we want, at least in the way that we want it. Resignation wears us out and takes away our motivation to persist. Even if we don't like our circumstances, in resignation, we will sabotage our efforts without knowing it.

We're likely to stop trying and we might find ourselves saying things like: *Why bother? They never listen. I'll just have to do it myself anyway.*

Instead of being clear about what we want in our relationships, our career and our hopes and dreams for the future, we don't take assertive action and we rarely ask for support where we need it.

Women who have been suppressed in some way or who have lived with gender inequality and mistreatment are likely to have slipped into resignation at some point. Resignation is a mood that can show us we care about something that matters to us. It's good to recognise what has been missing and to find more resourceful moods to operate from that are more likely to bring about change.

Signs of being stuck in resignation

- Telling the same story over and over again
- Using the word **but** which loops us back to a part in the story we repeat
- Ruminating over things we have little or no control over
- Having little or no ambition
- Not believing our voice will be valued

Resignation feeds inequality. It holds women back from having a strong voice and from getting a clear vision of what they want their future to look like, then going after it.

If we want to move on we have to let resignation know we no longer need its services. We can use the power in our pockets to bid it farewell.

Beyond the Resignation Trap

If we want to move beyond the Resignation Trap, we must believe it's possible to use our story for good. Awareness is power. When we are aware that we are stuck in resignation, we have the power to shift it by choosing more resourceful moods. And with that, we can turn the Good Girl Syndrome story into our own success story. We can change the old narratives for good.

Ask yourself: *How is resignation serving me for what I want to create in my life?* If the answer is that it's not, then choosing one of the moods listed, is going to be more useful to you, and give you the motivation to create change.

Experiment with choosing one of these moods instead:
- Acceptance
- Ambition
- Curiosity
- Peace
- Love

*Then the next important action is to believe and visualise what we **do** want, not what we don't want.*

– Jeanette

You are the author of the rest of your story

We have the power to reinvent ourselves. We are not designed to keep things as they are. If we lie stagnant, we don't progress as a human race. Reinvention is a self-authoring process.

In this process we get to decide how we want things to be for us in the future. If we're not looking toward the future and we haven't got a vision, we can ask ourselves if it's because we're living in the past.

> *No one can take our story from us. And no one can hold the pen and control how the next chapter of our story is going to go.*
>
> – Laura

We don't have the power to change the complex nature of the people around us, but we can make new choices for our own life, no matter how challenging things seem. There are possibilities waiting for us and they are just around the corner.

Our past may have left us with self-doubt or lack of confidence, and perhaps believing we're not worthy, but the truth is, we **are** worthy, and we do have a right to challenge the status quo. The question is: do we genuinely give ourselves that permission?

> *We can decide how we want things to be from now on. We can move beyond our past, and we can observe ourselves as strong, capable humans with dreams and equal rights to make a valid contribution to the world.*
>
> – Jeanette

Story – from shame to pride

After I'd been a sole parent for about two years, I visited a friend who lived nearby. I told her I still blamed myself for marrying my husband years before... and not leaving earlier when home felt unsafe.

I used to be like you. I never thought I'd be a single mum... I never thought I'd be one of those women.

My friend calmly took my hand and said, *But Laura, you **did** leave. And who are **those women**?* My mum was one of **those women**! Those women are **strong**. Those women are **amazing**!

She went on to say she had a work colleague who was a proud sole mum. Her work colleague used the fact that she was a sole parent with incredible time management skills and was dedicated to working hard to get the job! She saw herself as a valuable asset. In addition, she only wished to work for someone who valued her as an equal, with exceptional abilities. And she wanted an employer who was family-friendly.

My perspective changed in a blink. I'd imagined people seeing me as **less-than...** and while some people may think that way, whoever they were, they weren't my people! I'd not only done the best with what I had, I'd succeeded at breaking free when things were not safe... and had created a lovely new home for my kids.

I'd never treat other women or men who were sole parents with the harshness I'd treated myself. Through sharing part of my story, I was challenged to look at my story differently. I went from shrinking and lowering my head and confessing my status with a small voice to holding my head high and speaking with confidence and pride.

– Laura

This is a really powerful example of how a shift in perspective can change our outcome. It's also a great example of living by the values that are important to us, rather than sacrificing our own values trying to please everybody else.

POWER ACTION

Get to know your *her-story*

Pick one of your values – something that shapes your beliefs (in one single word). Write it down. Underneath that value, write down all the practices that are important to you.

Example:

Value: Family

Practices: Quality time together, kindness, respect for self and others

Now think about where that value came from. What makes it so important to you? Is it because you grew up with that value, or perhaps you saw this as an important value because you **did not** grow up with it? Write that down.

Who taught you? Write that down.

Would you like to keep it? Or would you like to replace it?

Write down yes/no and if you don't want to keep it what would you like to replace it with?

Key Points

- We all have deeply held perceptions and attitudes within our stories
- We all observe and perceive our experiences differently
- It's important not to get stuck in our past story
- Going in circles in our past story can show us we're resigned that nothing can change
- Story helps us to observe not just how the world is but how we want it to be
- We can listen to our story differently to see the invisible wall that may have kept us from the life we wanted
- We are the authors of our future life story

Chapter 3

Pull the Plug on People Pleasing
STEP INTO YOUR OWN AUTHORITY

> *As girls grow up and download what it means to be a culturally accepted 'good girl,' they learn to please others at the expense of themselves. They worry about protecting relationships – and what people think of them – at all costs.*
>
> – Rachel Simmons, *The Curse of the Good Girl: Raising Authentic Girls with Courage and Confidence*

We receive strong messages from the time we are little girls. These messages tell us it's important to be accommodating and nice, put others first and to be modest about our intelligence. How can that not affect our entire way of thinking and being?

Cordelia Fine academic philosopher psychologist and writer speaks about the wiring of our brains as girls and boys – and how it is not hard wired. It's absolutely changeable:

> *Our minds, society and neurosexism create difference. Together, they wire gender. But the wiring is soft, not hard.*

> *It is flexible, malleable and changeable. And if we only believe this, it will continue to unravel.*
>
> – Cordelia Fine, *Delusions of Gender*

Dependence on approval

It's always very interesting to observe children when they seek approval from their parents or other authorities in their lives such as teachers, aunties and uncles. Many of us have ourselves said it to a little girl: You're so *beautiful, and such a good girl!*

When we're little girls we were praised whenever we were good. This praise can become addictive, particularly when it validates us and makes us feel good about ourselves. It can leave us seeking more and searching for more moments that we can prove we are **good** or **smart** and it seems it's not okay just to be simply **enough**. The problem is many of us don't feel like we're enough, so where has society failed us? In many ways being a girl has conditioned us for approval.

Symptoms of being dependent on approval:
- People-pleasing
- Difficulty setting boundaries, hard to say no
- Low self-esteem
- Caretaking – being responsible for the emotions of others
- Caretaking – taking on the responsibilities of others
- Worrying about what others think
- Denying our feelings, needs, problems
- Avoiding conflict
- Having emotions such as anxiety, anger, resentment, hopelessness, shame

Lauren Martin speaks in her article 'Why Women Are So Hard On Themselves And Men Don't Think Twice' in *Elite Daily* about how primary school girls have learned to seek perfection. She says:

If you can recall, grade school was when we were brimming with confidence. It was before those teenage years set in, when we knew nothing but to take our looks and ourselves at face value. We were happy, unassuming and completely and utterly confident.

We were praised for our good behavior while we watched the boys of our class scolded and berated for their wild ones. As Carol Dweck, a Stanford psychology professor and the author of 'Mindset: The New Psychology of Success,' put it, we were praised for being perfect. That's where the long-term psychological issues set in. Instead of learning how to be yelled at, we learned to seek approval. Instead of practicing the art of risk taking, we practiced how to be perfect... psychologists now attest that failure and perseverance are the building blocks of confidence.

Being a Good Girl was a popular saying for many of us. This is the message many of us received from being praised. Boys have commonly been told they are being a bit rough but girls received disapproval for similar behaviours. Instead, girls have typically been told they were being too bossy and should be nice.

Being given constant praise for being Good Girls meant we weren't bad or naughty. It meant adults were happy with us, rather than disappointed or upset. It meant **approval**. Being good meant being **enough**.

That conditioning didn't suddenly disappear when we reached the rocky terrain of adolescence and became an adult. In fact many of us have taken on the importance of being everything to everyone as an important truth – and living through this very important role. So many of us have realised we're not happy doing that. It's our gut feeling telling us it has to change.

Continuing to think of everyone else first means giving up too much of ourselves – and that puts us in danger of fading into the background – so much that we completely lose our ability to know what we want... or how to get it.

What are we looking for? Are we looking for approval from others about our choices? And through their approval, does that mean we then approve of ourselves? Why should we wait for permission from others?

When we seek and depend on approval from someone else instead of ourselves, we are giving them the power to decide our worth... when we can give it to ourselves.

– Laura

Caretaking: Being responsible for others

Many women have felt they are responsible for everyone else's feelings and the things that are going wrong in the lives of others. Being a caretaker means absorbing the emotions of others, taking on their responsibilities and fixing their problems. Many of us have wanted to help other people avoid pain and suffering even if it means we will suffer in the meantime.

Playing the caretaker role can often mean we're jumping in and not allowing people to overcome their own pain and suffering. Unknowingly, being caretaker undermines another person's ability to overcome their own challenges and learn from their own emotional experiences.

Many of us have a nurturing side to us and we love to take care of others. There's nothing wrong with nurturing. However, it's important to notice when it's turning into the caretaker role.

Once we know the difference, we can then decide what actions we can take to be a supportive friend, mother, sister or auntie, without losing ourselves. The minute we assume and take on the responsibility of others or take on someone else's feelings, we risk being in sacrifice. This can even result in the person expecting of us what we've always given them. If we continue to oblige them, the cycle of approval will continue... despite any side effects of resentment.

Sacrifice is not service. Service is support and assistance. Sacrifice is obligation with very poor boundaries.

If we know inside ourselves that we're not responsible for the emotions, feelings and responsibilities of others, we will detox from seeking approval much faster. In turn, our self-esteem and confidence will naturally increase.

The more we put others and their feelings first, the more we put ourselves last. We can tend to avoid the things that really matter to us and whatever matters to other people becomes more important. It gives us a feeling of insignificance. When we matter less, our sense of positive self worth diminishes.

If we are in a loving and equal relationship, our past conditioning to seek approval may not impact negatively on the choices we make... but in an unequal relationship, our susceptibility to depending on approval puts our self-esteem and confidence at risk.

Knowing we have the power to observe where this outdated way of being came from, gives us different ways of observing and perceiving, and therefore the ability to change our reality.

> *Often women will say to me 'I don't want to speak up because I'm worried about someone disagreeing with me, or of causing an argument, or about upsetting people'. I completely understand that. I was reminded recently of just how much courage you need to speak up and share your truth, especially when you know the person listening might not want to hear what you have to say.*
> – www.theschoolofvisibility.com

Ditch the Apology

Studies have shown that women say **sorry** a lot more than men. Overusing **sorry** can hold us in a pattern of self-doubt. When we say I'm **sorry** we're actually saying **I shouldn't** have done that! It leaves us with a sense of regret and a feeling that we've done something wrong. When women are constantly trying to live up to the standard of being a Good Girl, if they do something seemingly wrong and **have to** apologise for it, they can be left feeling less-than.

> *I had to nudge someone's lunch bag over in the office fridge to make room for mine. I caught myself apologising out loud to a sandwich. I'm sure it still tasted fine, but my words did not.*
> – Sydney Beveridge, *HuffPost*, I am Woman, Hear Me Apologise: My Quest to Stop Saying Sorry all the Damn Time

Sydney adds, *Before we women even open our mouths, our words feel like an imposition rather than a contribution, and thus we feel we need to say 'I'm sorry' to cushion the impact. In fact, sometimes it seems like women apologise for just plain existing.*

When we do this, we weaken our message. Trying to cushion the impact of our boldness detracts from what we have to say and share with the world.

Seven things we should never apologise for

- Being confident and assertive
- Expressing our thoughts and opinions
- Expressing our feelings and emotions
- Being ourselves
- Sharing our passion
- Asking for help
- Taking time for ourselves

Sometimes we unknowingly set ourselves up for expectations beyond what we can physically give. Then if we fail to meet the expectations we can find ourselves apologising. For example, we give our time and energy to a friend, then the next week we're not able to and we feel a tug of war between doing it and saying no. We can't be in six places at once and yet guilt can overcome us in the blink of an eye. This is the **everything to everyone** story creeping in and letting us know we haven't given enough.

When you live with integrity and respect for others and yourself, you never have to apologise for who you are and the values you hold.

– Jeanette

Being our own authority

A Good Girl believes that expressing too much confidence and authority is not desirable. If she is even mildly assertive, she could be labelled as a bitch.

During our childhood we didn't have a choice but to give others authority over us because they were older, wiser and they were authority figures in our eyes, such as parents and school teachers.

We are taught to be humble and quiet – sit in the corner and don't speak, and be Good Girls. For a long time many of us have not been given a voice, so when we finally have one (thanks to many strong women who have come before us), we don't always know how to use it. If we make untrue assessments about ourselves, we are in conflict between showing up as confident and putting ourselves back in our place.

As we develop, we start to form our own unique views about the world, and take responsibility for our own thoughts, feelings and behaviours. It's assumed that by the time we're young adults it's assumed we can make our own choices and be our own authority. But sometimes we don't sufficiently learn the skills of taking the lead in our own life. This can be due to a range of environmental factors. The bottom line is, we can lose the sense of what it means to be in control of our life and therefore we look for people outside of us for the answers… not realising the answers are actually within us.

If we haven't learned to take the lead and if we don't recognise we have the authority to do whatever we want to do with our life, we can remain stuck in living life for someone else… or drifting along not knowing what we really want for ourselves.

Many women would rather take a back seat than disrupt the status quo. However, we know in our hearts this is not right and not good for us. So while we're in conflict between going along with things as they are and stepping outside the herd, we are susceptible to living with anxiety and fear. We apologise and try as hard as we can to take the front seat, but our nervous system is telling us not to disrupt the status quo.

Isn't it better to take a back seat than disrupt the status quo? *No* **it's not. Women absolutely have the opportunity to lead their own lives, to be their own heroes and to take back or**

gain their own authority. It's time to ditch the Good Girl life and start leading ourselves as strong women.

> *Self-approval and self-acceptance in the now are the main keys to positive changes in every area of our lives. Loving the self, to me, begins with never ever criticising ourselves for anything. Criticism locks us into the very pattern we are trying to change. Understanding and being gentle with ourselves helps us to move out of it.*
> – Louise Hay, *You Can Heal Your Life*

No more asking permission

How many times do we seek out the advice and opinions from others before we feel we can take action? Breaking free from Good Girl Syndrome means no longer asking for permission every time we do something.

Sometimes asking for advice or getting an opinion is courageous too – and totally necessary! But for many of us it can be a default we fall into that won't honour us for our own intelligence and experience. Some of us go a step further and ask several people for their advice and tick of approval.

> *It's better to get forgiveness than permission.*
> – Grace Hopper, computer scientist and navy officer, *Chips Ahoy*, July 1986

There's no doubt that Grace Hopper lived by what she said. She believed in following her good ideas, going ahead and doing them. This attitude took her a long way, especially for the time she was born...

Grace was born in 1906. She achieved several qualifications, including a doctorate in mathematics. In 1943 she got into the US Navy. Her project was to work on the very first large-scale computer, called 'Mark 1'. With hard work, she was the first person to be able to use it. She wrote programs for it and these programs meant the US army could crack codes sent by the other side. She didn't retire until 79 because her incredible expertise was hugely valued.

No more justifying and explaining ourselves

It's fine to share your dreams and the excitement that comes along with that, but you don't have to ask permission to have those dreams.
– Jeanette

A Good Girl feels obligated to always explain and justify her actions.

We can stand in our power and simply announce with certainty what we will be doing – if we choose to. Being unwavering in our decisions means there is less room for others to stop us or to prompt us to rethink our choices.

If friends and family have become used to us checking in with them and explaining or justifying ourselves when questioned, it could take them a while to get used to the new us – but if they don't like it, so what? We can practice caring less about what people think... until we discover we truly don't care. It's not that we won't care about **them**, it's just that we won't care about them giving us approval – and we know we are not obligated to justify ourselves.

The more sure of ourselves we sound, the more unshakable we become against second-guessing ourselves and being distracted from keeping our authority.

Life has taught us that we can't please everyone. And after all, it's not actually our responsibility to make everyone else happy and please them. We can play a part, but ultimately, their happiness is their paddock, their responsibility.

Story – I was suffocating

When I left my comfortable secure government job and started consulting back to the same organisation, the same creature comforts and income came with it. I was blissfully content in these comforts, however, something always felt like it was missing. I would go home at the end of a very long day – after what most would call a successful day – and my sentences would end with, *I won't be doing this forever*. Little did I know that eighteen months into consulting I would happily walk away and declare I wasn't going back. In hindsight, this wasn't very wise without an exit plan because when the income dried up, the creature comforts had to go.

Instead of giving up and finding more soulless contracting work, I decided to build a website and start coaching. The trouble was, I didn't know how to market myself, let alone who my ideal client was. For a couple of years I coached many clients for free. Financially there was a lot of strain.

During that time people around me had plenty of opinions. Well-meaning friends and family shared their concerns and made a lot of different suggestions about what I **should** do.

Go back to work, get more contracting jobs, they would say.

But this wasn't helpful. Being told what to do was stifling my creativity and quite frankly I was judging myself because of it. For a while I allowed it to affect me and felt guilty about my choices. But I never gave up. It would have been easy, but quitting wasn't in me. I knew from the depths of my soul, I had to stand strong and do what brought meaning and purpose to my life. I got to the point where I stopped explaining myself and justifying my decisions – and did what I wanted to do. It was when I was unwavering that I found freedom in my decision.

– Jeanette

Key Points

- The keys to pulling the plug on people pleasing:
- Observe when we are people pleasing
- Know we are not responsible for the emotions of others
- Know we are not responsible for fixing everyone else's problems
- Stop overusing the word **sorry**
- Give ourselves approval rather than seeking it externally
- Stop justifying and over-explaining ourselves

POWER ACTION

Watch some movies about girls and women who weren't Good Girls. Ask yourself what was more important to them and what they achieved by stepping out of outdated, sexist obligations.

Some you might like:

- Bad Mums
- I am Malala
- Hidden Figures
- Erin Brockovich
- Suffragette
- Brave
- The Eagle Huntress
- The Messenger: The Story of Joan of Arc
- Little Women
- Little Women Two
- Dream Girls
- Freida
- Nina
- The Women

It's really good to have conversations about controversial, disruptive or thought-provoking movies — have a movie night or a movie debrief!

Chapter 4

Being Enough

DITCHING PERFECTION IN A WORLD OF EXPECTATION

Why are women so judgmental about themselves?

There is growing pressure on women to achieve more than previous generations. As we move further away from our traditional roles and seek satisfaction in other areas of life such as career, our challenge to be enough is becoming increasingly complex. In a world where there is still a confidence gap between men and women, our latest challenge has become letting go of perfection and refusing to live with self-doubt.

Detoxing from Good Girl Syndrome means telling ourselves we are enough and it means no longer seeking perfection in everything we do.

When perfect is your standard

None of us are born with running shoes on, a diploma and a manual for how to do life. It takes a lot of life-learning and effort to accomplish new things. It's in giving things a go that we sometimes fall, pick ourselves up and have another go. That's the process it takes to achieve what we set out to achieve.

If we never **quite** believe we are good enough, we will find ourselves in search for perfection. Even when we know it's an impossible goal. Seeking perfection puts a cloud over all the things we've done well. No matter how much we are achieving, when we look through the lens of perfection, it's difficult to see how skilled and capable we actually are.

> *Perfection is the enemy of confidence.*
> – Katty Kay and Claire Shipman, *The Confidence Code For Girls*

Perfection knocks on the door and says, *Are you serious? Did you make that mistake yet again?* It leaves us comparing ourselves to the successes of others. And it can leave us feeling embarrassed and ashamed. It tells us why we might as well not bother applying for a position or start a business. It reminds us we're not as good as the next woman or man – and that we don't have what it takes.

On the other hand, lookin g through the lens of **being enough just as we are** allows us to see the things we've achieved. It gives us the ability to cope with challenges. Then when it's time to step into our confidence and go against the status quo, we will be ready to face any adversity that comes our way.

> *The only thing we really need to ask ourselves is if we love ourselves. Because self-love is the inner knowing that we are always enough no matter what.*

Story – Perfect is better than letting them down

I learned at a very early age to reach for excellence – which really meant perfection in the eyes of my father and his extremely high standards and expectations. It wasn't easy to feel like a failure because I was never measuring up to the type of person he wanted me to be.

Essentially, I was being told I wasn't enough as I was. I was either *fat, unfit, hopeless, a terrible mother, a stupid idiot* or *a stupid bloody bitch*. Being these things meant I had to try to change something

– something negative he assigned to me. This shaped the expectations and standards I had of myself. From this conditioning, I judged myself harshly and lived with the belief I wasn't enough. I often felt like a failure. I found it difficult to try new things and forge new relationships. Always pre-judging people's assessments of me, I hid myself away from talking to those I thought were better than me. Every time I was challenged, I would feel shame. Every time I got something 'wrong', I was embarrassed. I had to be perfect and I hated the thought of being exposed.

The search for an excellent result brought on a behaviour of desperation – of win at all costs. In one profound moment I realised what I'd been doing all my life, and that I could never measure up. Then another profound conversation with my mentor helped me to realise I was still doing it, even after that first profound moment. The second time around I stopped trying to search for results through the attitude of winning at all costs. I started to peel back the layers and believe in myself and accept myself just as I am. Finally I started to take more risks, and now, after a lifetime of playing small, I'm a speaker, a coach, an author – and I'm enough.

– Jeanette

When we strive for perfection we're not letting others down, we're letting **ourselves** down. The standards we set for ourselves may be because we've taken on the standards set by someone else. Desperately trying to live up to someone else's assessment of what it means to be enough, is not sustainable if we want to have the courage to live a life we love. As adults we can break that cycle by catching ourselves when we find we are striving for perfection.

> *No! Can't go back and make (the) same mistakes, must keep moving forward, and make new ones.*
> – Renee Zellweger as Bridget Jones in the movie: Bridget Jones's Baby, 2016

We are not perfect, we were never perfect and we will never be perfect. That's something to accept and celebrate because it frees us up to make mistakes without feeling shame, regret and embarrassment. The wonderful news about not being perfect is continually allowing ourselves to be human, and learn from mistakes.

The power of NOT YET

The phrase NOT YET is powerful

In her TED Talk 'The Power of Believing you Can Improve – The Power of Yet,' Carol Dweck tells us about a school in Chicago where students had to pass a certain number of courses to graduate. She says, *If they didn't pass the course they got the grade **not yet**.* She goes on to say how fantastic she thinks this is and states, *Because if you get a failing rate you think **I'm nothing, I'm nowhere**. But if you get the grade **not yet** you understand that you are on a learning curve.*

This is important as much in everyday life as it is in school or other learning institutions. We can replace the word **can't** with **not yet,** and in doing so accept ourselves as learners – not failures. By believing in the power of **not yet**, we'll be willing to learn new things and stick it out until we've accomplished what we set out to do.

Having a **not yet** mindset takes away the pressure of believing we have to reach lofty heights. In fact, it will not be about the lofty heights – it won't even be about us. **Not yet** will move us a little further away from negatively judging our abilities and from the pain of comparison.

For example, instead of saying, *I can't speak in front of an audience,* we can say, *I haven't spoken in front of an audience **yet**, but I'm going to learn how and then give it a go.*

And even when we don't believe we have the skills, knowledge or experience yet, it doesn't mean it's the end of the story. Skills can be gained, knowledge can be developed and every experience gives us insight and the ability to reflect and learn. **Not yet** keeps possibilities open for us.

We are always learning – and this is the power of **not yet.** Just because life isn't how we want it to be right now, it doesn't mean it can't be where we want it to be in the future. Just because we don't know how to do something, it doesn't mean we can't learn it. Just because our relationships haven't been healthy, it doesn't mean they can't be in the future.

When looking back is painful

Many women reach a stage sometime in their lives where they regret or question the choices they have made. Looking back, they start analysing how they lost themselves. Ruminating over the choices they didn't make, they worry that if they don't hurry up it will be too late. But it's never too late – many 60 + women are changing their life course or starting new careers. This is a reminder that when life is not quite as we want it to be, that we all have the means within us to do something about it, despite challenges or hardships.

To truly harness the power of **not yet,** we must stop looking at the past as an indicator of the future. The story of **I can't** takes away our power and shuts us off to new learning. It shuts down our inner belief that we are capable human beings... but **not yet** instills self-belief. It puts us into a growth mindset and gives us the confidence to create new and different experiences.

However, to do that means we really need to accept the existence of some things about our current circumstances. This does not mean we have to be satisfied. It just means we accept some things may have to remain the same for the time being. Acceptance gives us the headspace to take steps in order to shift out of old stories and start creating new ones.

I am enough can be our new story.

Life gives us the gift of wisdom. Wisdom is our teacher. Our past experiences are a reminder of all the things we have learned along the way, as well as the things we have achieved.

Wisdom can show us that we are strong, resilient and capable of overcoming adversity. It can give us the self-belief that we can pick ourselves up, even through the most challenging times.

The power of taking risks

Women are often in conflict between behaving in a way that society considers to be attractive... and taking risks or being competitive for their own sake.

New research suggests that adult women have less of an appetite for taking risks than men, and that girls suffer a significant drop in confidence during their teenage years.

A study published by researchers at the University of Stockholm found while pre-teen girls and boys are equally willing to take risks in high-stakes situations, girls are more likely to lose the confidence to do so by the time they reach adulthood. – The Independent UK News, Girls Lose Risk Taking Confidence By the Time They Reach Adulthood, While Male Confidence Grows

The risk is that excluding girls from the rough and tumble play that we typically assign as belonging to boys, discourages girls from taking risks. If girls have been discouraged from taking risks, while their brothers are cheered on for being daring and being tough, it denies girls the experience of falling and knowing they will be okay.

How do we take a risk when we're frightened of falling and failing, or worse still, we are frightened of becoming a **failure?** When we're laser-focused on getting things right, we are more likely to focus in on our past – the mistakes we made, and the beliefs we've adopted that convince us we're not smart or simply not enough. This focus makes it harder to see things that we've done well and learn by giving things a go.

Believing we're not good enough or not smart enough stems from beliefs. The human brain has developed to think rationally, and we use the frontal areas of our brain to come to conclusions. Our body on the other hand, has its own wisdom. It provides us with signals in the form of feelings and sensations. Together, these parts of the brain help us to make judgements and give us the ability to have an inner knowing that we can trust before our thinking brain kicks us into action.

Taking risks can continually build our confidence and change our response to future risks in positive ways. Each time we take a small risk we rewire our brains by creating new neural pathways. During this process of risk taking, we are building our confidence and expanding our world. Knowing that we've done it once before can give us the confidence to do it again.

> *Psychologists now attest that failure and perseverance are the building blocks of confidence.*
> – Lauren Martin, *Elite Daily*, Why Women Are So Hard On Themselves and Men Don't Think Twice

Taking risks means trusting and having faith that we will get through despite not being able to predict the outcome.

The more little steps we take, the more liberating it will be when we get past the fear, even when we don't necessarily achieve everything we set out to achieve. Stepping into new territories requires that we step outside our comfort zone. The more we attempt new things we might once have considered risky, the more we train ourselves to be courageous.

> *Courage will lead us out of our comfort zone and towards new experiences. It is the trial and error of these new experiences that continually expands our zone of learning – and our world.*

The advantage of growing up in a technological age means more teenagers and young people are harnessing innovation and beginning businesses. The technological age is not just for the young. More women in their 60s and beyond are changing their pathways and learning new skills. Some are launching life-changing nonprofits. Others are jumping into a new career or launching their own entrepreneurial ventures.

Every single new invention, company or life-changing product that exists first started with a risk at its inception. Each one has encountered teething problems and setbacks.

> *There's relief in knowing that lots of imperfect action gets far better results than waiting for perfection to arrive.*

Lead your own way forward

No one can tell us what to do or how to think.

We are the leaders in our own lives. We are our own authority. Even if there was a degree of inequality we were unfortunately born into and conditioned into, or someone specifically has treated us with disrespect – we were always born to be a leader of our own life. Just by being born means this is already in us.

The conflict going on inside, giving us mixed messages about when to go ahead and do something new or when to avoid the risk, can be unreliable. But there's rarely any one right answer – or a wrong one either. It can be just about the experience and what we discover along the way.

This is why it's important to take risks in spite of fear or confusion. Every new risk gives us new insight and new information for future decisions. It's about doing and learning things in action – not doing perfect actions.

> *There is power in believing that if we give something a go, trust will come.*
>
> – Jeanette

You are enough because you are you. Even if you change absolutely nothing, you are enough just as you are. You are enough when you make mistakes… and when you take risks and fall. Breaking free from expectations and limitations comes from really **knowing** you are enough.

No matter what, you never have to be perfect and you don't have to try and change who you are or what you do. By realising your choices are yours and yours only, you'll know that you are enough no matter what decisions you make – or what the outcome is.

POWER ACTION

What would you do if you knew you couldn't fail?

Write down all the things you can think about and don't filter them. Notice your responses. Don't judge them. If you're feeling uncomfortable, that's okay. Keep writing. The more you write, the more possible it will be to turn your vision into reality.

Key Points

- We are all learners – we cannot be failures
- Replacing the word **can't** with the phase **not yet** opens us up to being learners who are capable of anything
- Taking risks means trusting and putting faith in things with unpredictable outcomes
- You were never perfect, you are not perfect and you will never be perfect – accepting this saves you from shame, regret and embarrassment
- Learning builds trust. And self-trust allows us to take more risks

Chapter 5

Ditch Comparisons
EMBRACE YOUR UNIQUENESS

> *Perhaps it's got something to do with our past experiences of discrimination because of our gender or because we feel like we're in a minority, so then we are in a constant competition to come out on top.*
>
> – Adriana Bello, Why Women Compare Themselves to Each Other

The picture we paint of a perfect woman is unrealistic.

Do we really know who we are? Most of us could say we've been left searching for who we are for much of our lives. Society has held up a standard of what we should be, so it's no wonder we are comparing ourselves to those standards and constantly searching for our sense of self.

As a result we're often left making comparisons with other women. Women who we strive to be as good as and to achieve as they do.

We may have once had a picture in our heads as to what our lives would be like. The years pass. If life doesn't turn out as we dreamed it would, it's easy to regret what we didn't do and compare ourselves with others who have what we don't.

None of us is better than the other. There is beauty in our own uniqueness and in our imperfections. Despite there being millions of women in the world, none of us have an identical fingerprint. Doesn't that tell us we're meant to be unique?

Stay in your lane. Comparison kills creativity and joy.
– Brene Brown, *Rising Strong*

Our differences are what makes us who we are

In many ways we've turned our differences into roadblocks. We have all come from different backgrounds and we all have different experiences. Our families are unique combinations of people and their complexities. Each of us is hit with different challenges. Our bodies are different shapes and also go through different experiences such as childbirth or trauma. We each have different gifts and skills to share with the world. Our values vary. So do our ways of interpreting what we see and experience. Our interests and passions vary like the colours of a sunset.

Everyone has their own awesomeness, so it's not helpful to be envious of what someone else has. That's not to say we can't develop skills and knowledge to expand our own possibilities. However, we can also accept where we're at right now. Acceptance allows us to be learners, to see the possibilities and go after them. If we want something to be different, it's important to look at what we want, not what we haven't yet got that someone else has.

> *I accidentally discovered that gratefulness for another's blessings allows us to see more of our own.*
> – Jennifer Bleakley, The Battle of Comparison, shameonshanty.com

No one is living in perfection

When we see a beautiful picture that appeals to our eyes, our brain tells us we're attracted to it... and if we're not careful, comparison can set in.

Perfect portrait shots on social media and beautiful houses remind us of what others have that we don't. Movies and magazines can take us away on an envious fairytale of high profile people. It's these false images that entice us and suck us into the vortex of constant comparisons.

> *The grass may seem greener on their side of the fence – but maybe that's because you don't have your glasses on and can't see all the weeds and patches of dog pee.*
> – Laura

In reality, behind closed doors, the high profile people we see in perfect shots have the challenges and struggles as we do. They are just as likely to have piles of clothes all over the floor or acne on their less-than-flawless skin under makeup. No one is immune from a broken relationship or from having an ill or ageing parent. We are all vulnerable human beings with the same potential for pain and suffering.

Story – The red sports car versus the old station wagon

When Amy* drops off her children in her old car one morning, she pulls up next to a shiny red convertible. She sees a few parents turn their heads as her own car shudders and expresses its ultra-noisy desperation to go to a mechanic (which is where she is headed shortly). Embarrassment floods her cheeks.

She is very aware of the much newer models lined up in the car park. She compares her tired car and she compares herself to the other parents hopping out of their flashier cars. She finds herself saying to herself, *I don't belong here.*

Yet Amy has achieved the epitome of great, immeasurable achievement. She has spent thousands of dollars trying to protect her young children from ongoing family violence. On top of that, she's also funded needed psychology appointments to support them and she's also taken them on a five-day holiday earlier in the year to make memories with them. She's received no Child Support but still pays all school fees and all the big and little incidental costs. She could have spent her wages on buying a newer car but her highest value is family, which means prioritising what they most need – basic care and support. For now there is nothing left over.

As Amy puts her car into reverse, she hears the parent in the red convertible yelling at her own child in the backseat. The convertible abruptly begins to reverse before the little boy has even managed to properly shut the car door. Amy is reminded of what is much more important to her than a fancy new car.

*Name changed

Sonder

The Dictionary of Obscure Sorrows claims that **sonder** is: *The realisation that each random passerby is living a life as complex as our own.*

The briefest of conversations we have with people can show us how each and every one of us has our own story and sprinkle of hardships. For all we know, the lives of the people we have compared ourselves to may not be the picnic we assume. The woman we envy may have a very ill family member, her husband may never be home except to sleep... and maybe he has emotionally checked out. She may be experiencing bullying at work. And she may still be trying to pay off a massive debt that wakes her up at night.

And if people around us appear successful and happy, we can be failing to realise they may have had their own personal struggles to get there.

When we acknowledge the beauty in our differences and our various experiences and accomplishments, we can stand together and inspire each other.

Comparison is the thief of happiness.

– Laura Williams

Brene Brown says, *Letting go of comparison is not a to-do list item. For most of us, it's something that requires constant awareness. It's so easy to take our eyes off our path to check out what others are doing and if they're ahead or behind us. Creativity, which is the expression of our originality, helps us stay mindful that what we bring to the world is completely original and cannot be compared.* And, without comparisons, concepts like **ahead** or **behind** or **best** or **worst** lose their meaning.

Let's cheer each other on in our accomplishments, big and small.

Story – Taking a stance

I remember how much dad put my mum down. He called her stupid and was always yelling at her and demeaning her. She was a **stupid, bloody woman** in his eyes. She copped it, and we all copped it in whatever way he chose to dish it out to us.

He would come to watch me play basketball and yell if I wasn't playing up to his standards. He yelled a lot. He would never once tell me how well I'd played. Once, when I was 18, he was my coach. He was yelling at me the whole game – granted, I wasn't playing well, but who doesn't from time to time? As he pulled me off the court, the abuse got worse, until I finally stood up to him. *How dare you yell at me like this. Stop right now! You will never ever coach me again!* And he didn't.

Perhaps dad couldn't stop and he knew it. Perhaps he was ashamed. I don't know. But I do know that his expectations, standards and judgements had a huge impact on me. They led me to a life of negative self-judgements and chasing perfection. While I no longer hold the judgements and those standards, it took a lot of my adult lifetime to let go of them. Sometimes I still have to convince myself I'm enough because of how deeply ingrained they were.

Ironically, dad didn't meet reasonable expectations such as helping around the house, packing or lifting boxes into the car each time we moved or positive parenting. Mum was everything to everyone. Swim School manager, mother, taxi, cook, cleaner and removalist. No wonder she found it hard to be present with five daughters.

I'm not resentful or angry any more. I hold compassion in my heart for a man I never understood but always wondered what his expectations were on himself.

– Jeanette

It's not always easy to let go and make our own choices about what standards, expectations and judgements we take on. When as children we've lived in the shadow of huge expectations, we believe those in authority who have set those standards.

As adults we have a choice about what to believe and what to let go of. Perfection is something we can leave to car, aeroplane or space shuttle manufacturers.

In life we don't have to strive for perfection. We are unique and special just the way we are, even though it might not feel like that sometimes. By focusing on what others have that we haven't got, we lose sight of our own unique qualities. By focusing on the standards someone else sets for us, we miss our achievements.

Key Points

- Our differences are what makes us who we
- No one is living in perfection
- Everyone has their own struggles
- Living a life true to ourselves – without comparison – is our destiny

POWER ACTION

Accepting and loving you

Notice how many comparisons you make this week and what you're saying to yourself.

> Choose one positive thing about you. Something that makes you uniquely you.
>
> Write it down on post it notes and stick them on walls, mirrors and windows around the home.
>
> Notice how you feel as you read your notes.

Chapter 6

Delete Should

NO MORE RULES

The meaning of should
Modal verb: *You use should when you are saying what would be the right thing to do or the right state for something to be in*
– Collins Dictionary

If you are wondering what a modal verb is, the *Collins Dictionary* states that it is an auxiliary verb that expresses necessity or possibility. English modal verbs include *must, shall, will, should, would, can, could, may,* and *might*.

There is a narrative in society today that it's important to continue to reach higher. Unfortunately, this can often carry unrealistic expectations and standards.

> ***Should, must, have to*** *and **ought** to is the language of obligation*
> – Alan Seiler

At times it may be important to use **should** but not when it carries heavy expectations that diminish our power and authority and leave us constantly disappointed in ourselves. When **should** is used from a mood of anxiety, it is particularly difficult to move forward with ease, peace and confidence.

The residual effect of disappointment is blaming ourselves for things we believe we **should** and **shouldn't** have done – and being stuck in guilt. When we live with guilt, we can never really be happy and satisfied with our lives.

Guilt is often carried with regret. Regret means we're ruminating over things from the past we can't change – and getting stuck in these things. In regret and guilt we can never really have the freedom we yearn for, nor can we have the stillness of acceptance.

Detoxing from Good Girl Syndrome means setting ourselves free from the disappointment we have in ourselves. Forgiveness and acceptance are wonderful moods to empower us and shift away from disappointment. Why should we be constantly disappointed in ourselves?

The pressures of should

There's a lot of pressure in the word **should**.

It's a word that obliges us to:
- do better
- be better
- do something different
- or be something different

The world is so results-driven. Are we searching for ways to grow and become better human beings? Or are we maintaining the old, outdated story of reaching for perfection and overextending ourselves because we are women?

Having to juggle life, be everything to everyone else and live up to society's expectations and standards is hard and unstainable for a healthy life. When we don't believe we are measuring up, doing enough or being enough, the word 'should' is used to kick ourselves into action – but it can have adverse effects.

People have different opinions of what it means to be a good person. When people judge us, this is always an indication of how they think we should act according to **their** standards. Sometimes it doesn't show through their words, but it shows up strongly in facial expressions, tone of voice and general demeanor that we're somehow not measuring up.

How often do we judge ourselves and strive to change things about ourselves – **do better and be better?** It's as though we can't live with the pain of not measuring up.

The world has changed rapidly over the last fifty years and it's not about to slow down. Part of this rapid change puts pressure on us to change too. We're constantly trying to keep up with changes in things such as fashion, career, parenting, technology and consumables. Is there any wonder we say we **should**!

It's better to be a learner and not strive for some ridiculous standard. **Should** puts an enormous amount of pressure on us.

To reduce the pressure we can consider deleting the word **should** from our vocabulary.

The sneakiness of should

Imagine your car is on its last legs and you haven't got the money to buy a new one. It sets off a conversation of self-judgment. Your story may go something like this...

*I **should** have taken that job. If I had, I would have been able to afford a new car. I **shouldn't** have gotten into that relationship in the first place. If I hadn't I would be financially stable by now. I wish I had found someone better who treated me like an equal. I **should** have managed my money better. I'm **hopeless** with money. I'm hopeless. I'm going to end up on the street.*

Imagine your child is screaming up a cyclone in the supermarket. They're having the biggest tantrum anyone has ever seen. You're embarrassed and maybe even ashamed. The story may go something like this...

*I **should** have made her have more sleep last night. I'm always so bad at getting her to sleep and now she's so tired. I **should** be able to stop her throwing this tantrum. I **should** be a better mum. Why am I so bad at this? I'm a hopeless mother. I've failed. I'm a failure.*

See how sneaky this can be? *I'm a hopeless mother* is a Sneaky Declaration. Once we head down the rabbit hole of **should,** we usually find ourselves right at the bottom.

But it's the obligation in the first place that has us judging and running these Sneaky Declarations. If we didn't highlight the word **should**, would you have noticed how many times it was repeated in those conversations?

We are putting ourselves under obligation to do better, have better and be better, but in doing so we may inadvertently turn our **shoulds** into negative declarations. Remember, all declarations create our reality and shape our future. For example: **I'm a bad mother** stated one day can be a statement believed with conviction the next day.

Using **should** is common when we compare our situation to someone else's – for example different parenting styles, different ways to stay healthy, different areas to live, styles of homes, cars and reaching a certain financial status. We judge ourselves against others continuously, but we're all unique and we're all learners, so how are these comparisons relevant, and how are they serving us? *(See previous chapter on comparisons)*

The pressure of perfection that **should** so often evokes in us, is not sustainable.

Moods... and down the rabbit hole of should

We will always have an emotional response to our judgements. Whatever thoughts we have are going to trigger an emotional response. In falling down the rabbit hole of shoulds, we are likely to be experiencing emotions such as anxiety, jealousy, fear and regret. These are low-energy emotions, and when they're experienced over a long period of time they become moods. Then the moods themselves become a habit that is hard to break.

Should doesn't belong:
- When you sense pressure and expectation
- When the action is not a priority
- When you feel judgement
- When you feel anxious
- When it comes from a comparison
- When you feel jealous, regretful and fearful

Every time you judge someone you risk judging yourself.
– Jeanette

A big indicator to remove **should** is when our language involves negative self-judgements. We can take more decisive actions and feel more in control of our lives when we allow ourselves to question **should.**

A place for should

There is a place for **should** when it comes from a creative place and brings on something exciting, new, wonderful or positive and if it leads us to take actions that feel right. If we feel aligned to the actions behind the words right away, we're probably on the right track.

For example, a friend says to us, *We should go for a bush walk,* or when we're thinking about learning something new and we say, *We*

should *do some research*. It's healthy as long as the mood we experience around it is also healthy.

If we truly want to try new things, it's important not to let the Resignation Trap, anxiety and fear get in our way. In this case we can replace **should** with **I will**. Declaring something by beginning with **I will**, turns the words into declarations and cuts off hesitation and self-doubt. Trying new things pushes us out of our comfort zone. Even if we don't like being out of our comfort zone, we have to stretch ourselves and never give up.

Story – The fence post

When I was sixteen, my seventeen-year-old cousin came to visit. He and his brothers came from a sheep farm. What we loved to do is race around the paddocks in an old car – a 'paddock' bomb as we called it. It was a little Morris Major. My parents had been passionate about my brother learning to drive early and thought that the paddocks were the best place to do so. On this occasion I jumped in the front seat. My cousin sat in the passenger seat and my brother sat in the back.

Quickly, I got the car up to speed. We laughed and were carefree as we zoomed along. I sensed my cousin hanging on (most likely for dear life!). I knew the track well. Third gear was my favourite to coast around the forest. Down the hill, I didn't slow down much. This time I took the turn a bit too fast and instantly slid out sideways in the dirt. BANG. The side of the Morris slammed hard into a fence post. With our hearts pumping, we got out, recovering from the shock – and surveying the damage. Oops. The fence post was well and truly broken and rendered useless. Our cows were going to get out. My cousin remarked in amusement that I'd gone pretty darn fast around the last corner.

He never used the word **should** but I found myself saying, *I should have gone slower. Oh, no, what's Dad going to say?*

My cousin was unflappable. Calmly he said, *What your father doesn't know won't hurt him. Where can we find another post? We can fix it.* Before I knew it, a new post was put in and the wire repaired.

Taking out a fence post was a learning experience. From then on, corners were respected. And I also learnt that laughing at myself and fixing things was a better use of time than pondering under the judgement of any shoulds.

Ever since, I have had a few battles with the word should. Why have I been so hard on myself? I shouldn't be!

As the author of your future story you're making constant adjustments to the way you navigate your life. Sometimes change feels unfamiliar and uncomfortable. Any negative assessments or expectations you hear yourself saying are not the truth. We invite you to always remember the only expectations you have to live up to are yours.

Failure is a story. You are not a failure and you never will be. You are a learner. Be a rebel – set yourself free from dumb rules and expectations.

Next time you catch yourself saying **I should** (or **I shouldn't**) be doing this or that, we invite you to take a few deep breaths, put your hand on your heart and feel gratitude for the strong amazing woman that you are. Give thanks to yourself for standing up against the status quo and stepping out into the world without self-judgement.

POWER ACTION

Observe Should
Observe yourself saying **should** or **have to**
Sit with it without judging it – just observe it
Let the **why** come to you

Question if there is a place for it:
When you sense something's a bit 'off'
When the action is not a priority
When you feel judgement in your gut
When you feel anxious
When it comes from a comparison
When you feel jealous

... then you can start to turn **shoulds** into curiosity for your future and what you want it to look like.

Key Points
- When we use the word **should**, we may be putting undue pressure on ourselves
- **Shoulds** leads us into harsh judgement of ourselves
- **Shoulds** can lead us into anxiety, jealousy, fear and regret
- Remove **should** when it involves judgement of ourselves or others
- There is a place for **should** when it comes from a creative place

Chapter 7

Emotions

YOUR INNER GUIDE

The ripple effect from women being viewed as emotional and too sentimental through generations has given us a poor understanding of the role of emotions and their intrinsic value.

Too much emotion to lead

It wasn't that long ago that influential men claimed that women's emotions took over their ability to reason and contribute. As a result, women were forbidden to vote in elections and discouraged from traditional male dominated industries, such as science, finance and emergency services. This reinforced the concept that being emotional meant there must be something wrong with us. This misinformed and inaccurate understanding of emotions has done a disservice to women and men.

(Yet) a new analysis from the Georgetown University Center on Education and the Workforce (CEW) suggests that, despite the undeniable progress, female candidates continue to face a significant headwind that has absolutely nothing to do with their abilities or qualifications: **13% of Americans—or roughly**

one in 10—still believe men are better 'emotionally suited' for politics than women.

– *Fortune*, 13% of Americans Think Women Are Less 'Emotionally Suited' to Politics Than Men,
Kristen Bellstrom, 16th April 2019

It is assumed women are too soft, emotional or hysterical for leadership roles. Most career paths have been developed with men's lives in mind.

– Julia Gillard, 2012, in her speech about misogyny

For centuries there was an opinion that people must control their emotions. Unfortunately, emotional control has led us to devalue the ability of our emotions in giving us insight and new learning.

> *As much as our emotions can feel incredibly uncomfortable at times, they are not your enemy. In fact, they are your ally and your inner guide to everything you think, feel and do.*
>
> – Jeanette Mundy

The human struggle with emotions

Both men and women have been left emotionally illiterate. This means that many of us have limited ability to name our emotions and to know how they feel in our bodies. The potential downfall is our failure to understand their intrinsic value to us and to trust their central role in our lives. Therefore, when we have an emotional experience, we find it hard to cope.

When women are stuck in gender conditioning, they often experience associated emotions such as sadness, anguish, fear, shame, guilt and regret. Some women think that if they let themselves experience an emotion they might get trapped and overwhelmed by it. So they find themselves trying to be strong and stoic, saying things like, *What good will it do me to let myself be sad?* What they don't often realise is that there is a lot to learn from our emotional experiences.

There is a gradual recognition of the importance of emotions and emotional intelligence, but many of us are still relying on rational and logical thought alone. We use our thinking brain to make sense of the world – and when we find ourselves repeating the same old patterns of behaviour, we judge ourselves for not getting it right.

It's generally not a compliment to be referred to as emotional, and yet having emotions is a crucial part of being human. To be human is to be constantly living in emotional experiences. We can't live without emotions and they go hand in hand with logic.

Dan Newby and Lucy Lunz, *The Unopened Gift, A Primer in Emotional Literacy* says, *We (society) believe they (our emotions) are not trustworthy and that they compete with or are in opposition to thinking and logic. We see them as the opposite of reason and generally believe they need to be 'gotten out of the way' in order to 'think clearly'.*

We believe they are fixed or at least very difficult to change and that they can only be changed with professional help. Our principal way of interacting with our emotions is to control or manage them, or at least to try. Beyond that, we often fear their power and believe life would be better if we had fewer of them.

Both men and women have the ability to experience all kinds of emotions, but because we've typically associated men with strength and courage, and women with empathy and compassion we've assigned certain emotions as more acceptable for each gender. No matter what our gender, being human means we have the ability and right to have all kinds of emotional responses to life events and circumstances.

There are certain emotions connected to the belief that we are less than others, or that we are not enough just as we are. Self-doubt, worry, guilt, dejection, resignation, resentment and shame, to name a few. Comparing ourselves to others, treating ourselves as though others are more important and hold more authority than us means shrinking down in certain emotional experiences instead of learning **from** them. Without taking our own concerns into consideration, we find ourselves complaining, comparing and judging – and so often judging ourselves.

Doubt is an emotion. **Self-**doubt is the belief that in some way we personally don't measure up. The emotion of doubt means *I am unsure*. Self-doubt means *I am unsure of myself*. It makes us hesitate, prolong action and avoid certain situations, especially if they are new to us.

Living as a Good Girl results in self-doubt. It stops us from asking for what we want, and what we need because we don't believe we have the right or the ability to have the necessary conversations.

Emotions are not just words on a page to understand. They're experiences that show our concerns – what's really important to us. Of course if we've been conditioned to be Good Girls what matters to us isn't as important as what matters to everyone else.

Emotions need an opportunity to be felt – and opportunities to move in and through them. It's not until we give our emotions a seat at the table that we truly know deep down what our concerns are and how to take care of them. Imagine if we continue pushing these insightful, intuitive feelings away?

The darker side of emotions

Can you remember the last time someone told you to pull yourself together or to stop being so sensitive? Could a possible translation be that you experienced a human emotion the other person was not comfortable witnessing?

This is a common experience for those of us who have lived with inequality or mistreatment. People in general find it difficult to handle someone who is experiencing elevated emotions. Someone who assumes more power may try to convince us that our emotional experiences are wrong.

Gaslighting is a common tactic to convince someone to doubt themselves and their reality. One example is someone using intimidating behaviour (let's say they are yelling and throwing items near us)... then when we tell them we feel intimidated, they say, *You're being too sensitive.*

Fear

Due to inequality and mistreatment for centuries, women globally have had to run away from threats and often hide for fear of being harmed. Fear and anxiety is the human body's fight or flight responses for protecting us and taking care of our safety. How are we supposed to get our emotions under control when we're trying to protect ourselves? If our body is keeping us safe as it's designed to do, it wouldn't allow us to stay in control of our emotions.

Anger

Anger is the human body's response to stand against and protect ourselves from something we don't like. Many women, as part of Good Girl conditioning, have learned that it's not polite to be angry. To be a Good Girl often means to be a lady and ladies do not get angry, they are just mildly cross. Anger is a more direct message that something is really off here. It's important to recognise it has its place when we or someone else has been mistreated.

> *Anger gives us the ability to see injustice and call it out for what it is.*
> – Jeanette

Feeling angry gives us an opportunity to explore how to get really clear about our concerns, rather than pushing them down and ignoring them, to find resourceful ways to channel the anger. This does not mean we have to go into a conversation while angry or beat someone over the head with a stick in rage.

We have so much to learn from our anger. Women across the globe are finding resourceful ways to channel their anger, and making a really big difference in the world. Deciding which emotions and which actions will serve us is emotional management – not emotional control. Courage, determination, indignation and ambition are powerful emotions that disrupt the status quo and bring about change.

Emotional triggers

Our emotional memories are stored throughout our body in tiny little nerve cells waiting to be triggered. They are part of our stories, accumulated from a lifetime of experiences. You can't push them away, jump over them, or go around them.

As we view the sunset from a rocky cliff overlooking a coastline, hear the sound of the waves, and feel the breeze on our face, we experience an emotion such as peace, calm, awe, happiness or gratitude. In the future, when we remember that moment, the experience can trigger the same emotions. Our emotions shape our interpretations and how we see things.

If someone interrupts us from something we're doing, we might experience frustration and annoyance. If we haven't processed that frustration and annoyance, we will likely have the same emotional trigger when we are interrupted in future.

Instead of pulling away from negative emotional triggers, we can validate them. We are emotion-**ing** beings, which means we are always taking action in and through our emotions. Therefore, we don't have a choice but to live with them – and sometimes that means stepping into the force of an ocean gale and riding the surging waves of the storm.

We can accept the emotions that are a part of our past, talk about them, and decide if they're serving us for what we want to create. This is more than simply validating our emotions, it's validating our **concerns** and the things that really matter to us, which is why we're experiencing the emotion in the first place!

> *You might as well give your emotions a seat at the table – they're going to annoy you until you pay attention!*
> – Jeanette

Our emotions are brilliant teachers

We can rely on our emotions to bring attention to our deepest concerns. They can be a roadmap to help us find our way to take care of the things that matter most to us. The question we can ask ourselves is: *Are we ready and willing to be an emotional learner?* Learning about and through our emotional experiences can absolutely change the quality of our life for the better.

Positive ways we can think about our emotions:
- Have compassion and acceptance of all our emotional experiences
- Trust our intuition when something is bothering us
- Choose resourceful emotions – ones that support us take care of what matters to us

Changing our emotions means changing our responses to our experiences.

All emotions have an underlying thought such as, *I'm always interrupted. It's so annoying, nothing I say ever makes a difference. I might as well not bother. This is the way it is in our house.*

The thoughts we have are our judgements and opinions about the experience, that trigger the emotions. For example, when we make the assessment that we're looking at a beautiful sunset we feel the emotions of happiness and awe. Or when we make the assessment that someone should have been helping us, we feel the emotion of frustration or anger.

Part of being an emotional learner is to be able to connect our thoughts and emotions together.

> *All our thoughts carry emotional, mental, psychological, or spiritual energy to produce biological responses that are stored in our cellular memory.*
>
> – Caroline Myss, *Anatomy of the Spirit*

When emotions help us take action

Imagine we are looking out the window into our backyard. We see the garden looks a mess and the weeds and grass are one metre high. We feel **frustrated** that we have let it get that bad. **Frustration** prompts us to the fact that we have a standard and the backyard and garden is not meeting that standard. We **wonder** what we could do about it. **Wonder** gives us the creativity to think about how we want it to look. As we start to come up with things such as mowing, weeding and planting, **ambition** kicks in, and we are motivated to take action. Motivation gives us the drive to seek what we need: time, money, plants and so forth. The plan is in action. While frustration was the initial driver, if we remained in frustration it would be less likely that we would activate such a creative plan.

If we let ourselves stay in resignation and hopelessness that the garden was too big a job to fix, we might keep ruminating over it but doing nothing about it. On the other hand, if we activate the emotion of ambition we're more likely to come up with ways to get it done.

> *Having a daily ritual or practice of gratitude, joy and calm can change our personal experiences and overall way of being.*
>
> – Jeanette

Story – How grief was pushed away

I remember when my grandfather passed away and we kids weren't allowed to go to the funeral. Not only that, no-one in my family helped me through my grief. I remember being really sad the day I found out, and going down to the local telephone booth to call my friend. She was the only one I spoke to and shared how I felt about it. I remember thinking I just had to get over it after that call. I loved my grandfather and I was so sad when he died. While I did recover from my grief, I never got to speak to anyone about the circumstances surrounding his death, and I remember feeling so uncomfortable around my grandmother in her grief. I also never saw my mum sad. My dad was the one who broke the news, and I just had to assume mum had gone to see my grandmother and must be very sad. She never once spoke a word about it to me. I learned that grief had to be hidden.

As I grew up I purposely went to any funeral I could get to, so I could experience grief and pay my respects. For this reason I felt it was important. I'm lucky that I do know how to feel and express grief and sadness now, because in front of certain people or in certain circles, for a long time I had avoided it at all costs. The message was, *I must be strong*. My perception was that sadness meant weakness – and I was not going to show weakness!

– Jeanette

Trust your emotions

Emotions help us live in alignment with our values. They help us make better judgements and have better relationships. They help us identify our concerns, and bring more joy into our lives. They also help us see the world in different ways.

When we have the courage to sit in them and give them a voice, we can begin to look at them – not as though they are evil or taboo – but as though they are very handy resources which are internally a part of us, we can begin to innately trust them. None of us can suddenly know how to do this. Emotional learning, and emotional trust is a learning curve, just as learning anything else is.

Trusting is knowing that every single emotional experience we have, is there for a reason. Then we can ask ourselves how our emotions and thoughts together are shaping our experience.

Story – Emotions with a message

I told someone how I wanted to solve a problem I was facing. Her face turned pink like a ripening tomato. She lectured me about 'the facts' as she saw them. I tried to explain myself and yet I agreed that one part of her perspective could well be right. After the conversation a sickening feeling stayed in my gut. As soon as I got into the car, I felt tears wanting to escape. Argh. What was wrong with me?

Nothing. I was feeling guilt, shame and self-doubt.

The next day, I reflected on what had happened. The queasy, sickening sensation was still there. I asked myself what emotions I was feeling. As the emotions triggered me, I realised she had definitely been judging me – she was telling me what I should and shouldn't do. I didn't have much room in the conversation to speak. I came to the conclusion that there was an obvious power imbalance in this relationship.

As I reflected on the conversation, I began to trust my own judgements and shame melted away.

This was a terrific learning experience as it taught me to listen to and trust my body's responses much sooner! And in the future, instead of rolling over like a submissive puppy as I had done any times in the past, I would politely and assertively announce that I felt uncomfortable with the way I was being spoken to – and put an end to the conversation.

– Laura

Every single emotion and emotional experience you have is valid and is there to teach you something. You don't have to push them away, and you don't have to hide them. You don't have to listen when someone attempts to invalidate your emotions. No one else is in your shoes, so it's not up to them to decide whether your emotions are valid. Equally it's not up to them to judge you. The beauty of emotions are the feelings you get and the sensations you feel throughout your body, and that's because these are the messages they bring you.

Know that you have a right to feel and to explore what they are there to tell you.

> *By recognising our emotions, naming them, figuring out what matters to us, then deciding which emotions are going to serve us for what we want to create, we can find more resourceful ways for moving forward and become unstoppable in our endeavours.*

POWER ACTION

What is your experience with emotions?

We all grow up understanding and experiencing emotions differently. It's interesting to notice particular emotions that were considered acceptable to express within our families, and those that were not.

Which emotions do you think you were you encouraged to experience as a child?

See if you can name about three to five emotions that feel familiar to you or that you're comfortable experiencing. If you can't think of any right now, reflect on this in the next couple of weeks and see what comes up for you.

Which emotions were you not allowed to experience as a child?

See if you can name a few emotions you'd rather avoid, don't know how to experience, or have never experienced. If you can't think of any right now, reflect on this in the next couple of weeks and see what comes up for you.

If it was possible for you to experience them, what difference would that make in your life?

This action is particularly helpful when you're trying to process something that you're stuck on. Often it's the emotions we were unable to express or feel that are the ones we least understand.

Key Points

- Emotions are the driver behind every action we take
- Many people have lived with people who have invalidated their emotions
- We don't have to move our emotions out of the way to think clearly
- Our emotions are our greatest teacher
- We need to know how to name our emotions to learn about them
- We can become very powerful observers of our emotions
- Emotions helps us process our challenges and create breakthroughs

Chapter 8

Overwhelm and Burnout

FIND YOUR INNER CALM

The meaning of burnout
Exhaustion of physical or emotional strength or motivation usually as a result of prolonged stress or frustration.
– Merriam-Webster Dictionary

Overwhelm can hit when we are overloaded with information, responsibilities, demands and stressful circumstances – and when we are unsure if we can handle it all. It's almost a trend that as women we must juggle a million tasks like a badge of honour.

Overwhelm and stress in little bursts may not be detrimental to our health and wellbeing. However, if we don't take action and continue to live in a state of overwhelm, we are at risk of burnout. With the weight of expectations, many of us run ourselves into the ground – and yet are shocked when we finally discover we're burnt out.

Overextending

We expect a lot of ourselves. Sometimes too much. How many of us are rushing around like ants before the rain falls, with our paid job, running a business, caring for those around us and running around trying to fit in extra activities – and trying to fit all this into a 24-hour day!

There is a social narrative that women are good at multitasking. We have been led to believe it is a special multitasking ability. But we've actually had the wool pulled over our tired eyes. A recent study shows that women are **no** better at multitasking than men – it puts cognitive strain on the brains of **both** men and women.

Women aren't better multitaskers than men – they're just doing more work, states Leah Ruppanner when she refers to the results of a study that shows women in partnerships are generally doing a lot more housework and childcare on top of having a paid job… and their mental health is therefore being greatly impacted.

Overextending ourselves can be the result of taking too much on. Because society places so much emphasis on having to work hard in order to get somewhere in life, we can become quickly trapped into this story of overextending.

> *It's time we took OFF the badge of honour for overextending ourselves. It's time we valued ourselves as much as we value everyone else – and simplified our lives. Doing this will reduce stress. Reducing stress will mean overwhelm can't hang around. Without overwhelm, burnout doesn't get a look-in!*
>
> – Laura

Many of us believe we are still required to continue to uphold our traditional roles and cram in the 'privilege' of self expression and career aspirations in our 'spare' time. It's not a privilege, it's a right and part of necessary self-care for everyone.

These deeply ingrained attitudes run through the fabric of our being. What is the story behind this? Are we believing that to get somewhere in life it means we have to take on the world and struggle in the process? Changing the story means changing perceptions of what it means to be a woman.

Struggling has a negative energy attached to. It's important to find a balance that works for us to ensure we maintain our energy and avoid burnout. This requires us to be clear about our roles, responsibilities and commitments.

> *Instead of drowning in overwhelm, we can acknowledge the message it is telling us and give ourselves the care we need to recharge... well before burnout.*
>
> – Laura

The stress response

Our brain responds to stress by releasing stress hormones, such as adrenaline and cortisol. This response is commonly known as fight or flight. It's the brain's way of helping us avoid danger or urgently need to accomplish an important task in record time.

Dr Nadine Burke Harris speaks about this in her TED Talk 'How Childhood Trauma Affects Health Across a Lifetime'. She talks about the helpfulness of our stress response in a stressful situation...

Imagine you're walking in the forest and you see a bear. Immediately, your hypothalamus sends a signal to your pituitary, which sends a signal to your adrenal gland, that says **'Release stress hormones! Adrenalin! Cortisol!'**

And so your heart starts to pound, your pupils dilate, your airways open up, and you are ready to either fight that bear or run from the bear.

*And that is wonderful **if you're in a forest and there's a bear.** But the problem is what happens when the bear comes home every night, and this system is activated over and over and over again, and it goes from being adaptive, or life-saving, to maladaptive, or health-damaging.*

According to Dr Jo Dispenza, educator in neurology, neuroscience, brain function and chemistry, cellular biology, memory formation, *Most people spend 70% of their life living in survival and living in stress, so they're always anticipating the worst case scenario from a past experience.*

He goes on to say, *They're selecting the worst possible outcome and they're beginning to emotionally embrace it with fear and they're conditioning their body into a state of fear – do that enough times and the body has a panic attack without you – you can't even predict it because it's programmed subconsciously.*

Overwhelm is a condition of the body that involves associated emotions such as fear and anxiety. The longer we stay in a state of overwhelm the more familiar it becomes.

Dr. Jo says, *The familiar past will sooner or later be the predictable future.*

He adds that many of us keep recalling the event and then become addicted to the same emotions we experienced during the event. The same hormones are produced every time we are reminded of that event. This is our body repeatedly believing and living the same past experience.

A little bit of stress is not a bad thing. It prepares us for challenging situations. However, too much stress has a harmful impact on the body. Caroline Leaf, author, neuroscientist and researcher, sums this up by saying that stress has a horrific, negative impact on our nervous system, our heart, immune system and digestive system.

It (burnout) occurs when you feel overwhelmed, emotionally drained and unable to meet constant demands. As the stress continues, you begin to lose the interest and motivation that led you to take on a certain role in the first place. Burnout reduces productivity and saps your energy, leaving you feeling increasingly helpless, hopeless, cynical, and resentful. Eventually you may feel like you have nothing more to give.

– helpguide.org

Signs that overwhelm could be leading to burnout:
- Feeling exhausted and drained
- Headaches, pain in muscles
- Feel like a failure, **not enough**
- Feeling depressed and unmotivated
- Hopeless, negative state of mind
- Detaching from people

Overwhelm and burnout shows up as stress in our bodies. When it does not **ease**, we are at risk of it manifesting into **disease**.

The association between stress and disease is a colossal 85%.
– Brian Luke Seaward, *Managing Stress: Principles and Strategies for Health and Wellbeing*

No system of the body is spared when stress is running rampant... being aware of the toxic pathway of stress, which targets various systems and organs along the way, is important.
– Dr. Caroline Leaf, *Who Switched off my Brain: Controlling Toxic Thoughts and Emotions*

Three powerful ways to reduce overwhelm:
1. Simplicity
2. Wonder
3. Gratitude

1. Simplicity

> *There is power in simplicity. When things feel unbearably overwhelming, decrease the noise and busyness in our lives. For our minds to truly recover and refresh, it needs peaceful rest.*
>
> – Laura

To simplify our lives, we need to change the story we live in. We can reframe our thoughts to believe there is a way to reduce overwhelm. As a result of that reframing, we can reassess and reduce the responsibilities and commitments we've made.

Make a plan
Draw a circle. Now draw a much smaller circle inside it. Your life and your activities represent the large circle. Now imagine shrinking your world so that it fits into the smaller circle in the middle. This is about eliminating what doesn't matter, and only holding onto what really, really matters.

Cut down our workload
It's easier said than done, but if we can, cut corners and don't be perfect. We can streamline our responsibilities. Find support and be prepared to invest in it. Fall in love with the word **no**. When people ask for our help, we can give ourselves time to think about it before making a commitment. We can ask ourselves if helping is the best choice for us in this moment.

Delegate
What can we ask someone else to do? Many of us are used to having people ask us to take on tasks – or used to other people assuming we will take on numerous tasks. Part of delegating tasks to others involves letting others do a less perfect job, letting them make mistakes, and accepting that mistakes are part of life. Sometimes letting go enables others to step up. It also means learning from each other. It's not a role of any one person to take on everyone else's concerns so they can put their feet up or just do the fun stuff.

(See Chapter 11 – Set Clear Boundaries, for more on this)

Simplify your options
According to David Levitin in his book *The Organized Mind: Thinking Straight in the Age of Information Overload*, in 1976 the supermarkets stocked an average of 9,000 items. Now they typically stock around 40,000 items. There will be times we may want to analyse twenty varieties of pasta sauce – but not when we are on a mission to reduce overwhelm. Create lists for your priorities – for your time and for grocery lists, lists for work tasks. Keep life simple by removing choices. Simplifying your options is like a decluttering of the brain so that there's less that your brain has to process.

Get a good night sleep
Sleep is how we heal and repair our bodies. Every time we go to sleep, our body gets a break. Our breathing slows and relaxes. Hormones, stress levels and energy levels reset. Our immune system is given a boost and inflammation is reduced. Our brain gets to work to process the day's experiences, including any stress or overwhelm. Sleep is where our dreams come to life and our vision for the future can show up to us. When we wake from a restful sleep, our brains will be ready to function.

Create a morning ritual
Start each day with daily rituals. This will create new healthy habits and significantly reduce the chance of overwhelm overtaking our brain and body before the day begins. A ritual helps us get into the habit of putting ourselves first and having more positive experiences.
- Meditate: fill our minds with peace and positivity
- Move: exercise to release feel good chemicals like serotonin and endorphins
- Mood: pick the mood that creates positive experiences
- Intention: choose how we want to interact with ourselves and others
- Positive thinking: Reframe negative thinking into positive thinking

Connect to people
When we connect with other positive people we're more likely to experience uplifting moods because we're doing things we enjoy. It helps us to get some separation from the overwhelm. People can

give us fresh perspectives, help us laugh and bring joy to our day. Community and connection is vital to our wellbeing. Find community and ask for ways to help share the load.

Accept the things that are out of your control

There are some things that we can't change and are out of our control. Accepting what we cannot change can prevent us from ruminating. It will allow us to move through and past circumstances that have been holding us back. Acceptance is a mood which allows us to move toward a positive future.

All of us want to feel at peace. Peace means **all is well** with the world. In peace we move with ease and rest without worry. It's aligned to tranquility and serenity. Acceptance allows us to move into peace and sets the mood for a positive future.

Detox from screens

We can control our phone rather than allowing it to control us. Find moments in the day to take a technology break. Perhaps when it's on charge is the time to walk away. Put it on do-not-disturb mode. We can take a break from watching the news and from scrolling through social media. Switching off grounds and re-energises us.

Embrace peaceful places

Spend time in quiet places, such as a park, a forest, a beach or simply in our bedroom snuggled under the doona. We can listen to peaceful music. Light candles. Dim or turn off lights. Meditate. Think about the wonders of life.

> *In the midst of great things, we literally dress rehearse tragedy. Instead, use that sensation as a reminder to be grateful. Practicing gratitude leads us into joy.*
>
> – Brene Brown, The Call To Courage, *Netflix*

2. Gratitude – the secret sauce to combat overwhelm and burnout

> *Gratitude is appreciation that has finally struck the heart... Walking the grounds of gratitude I stumbled upon the palace of happiness.*
> – Brendon Burchard, *The Motivation Manifesto: 9 Declarations to Personal Power*

Gratitude is the belief that life is a gift. We can't just **say** we're in gratitude, we have to **experience** it.

Gratitude frees us from being stuck in a spiral of stress – and overwhelm that can result from it. When we are concentrating on all the things we are grateful for, including gratitude for how far we have come and what we have, overwhelm can be like a visitor who doesn't step inside our front door. Overwhelm may visit to send us the message that we need to simplify *and* focus on the *good* things in our lives.

Studies have shown that gratitude is one of the keys to joy and an optimistic mindset. One study showed that writing gratitude letters (that weren't necessarily sent in the mail) gave the writers a greater sense of joy and positivity. The doctors who conducted that study said:

When you write about how grateful you are to others and how much other people have blessed your life, it might become considerably harder for you to ruminate on your negative experiences.

– Joel Wong, Ph.D. And Joshua Brown, Ph.D, Indiana University, *How Gratitude Changes Your Brain*

When disaster strikes, gratitude provides a perspective from which we can view life in its entirety and not be overwhelmed by temporary circumstances. Yes, this perspective is hard to achieve, but my research says it's worth the effort.

– Robert Emmons, Ph.D., University of California, the world's leading expert on gratitude, *How Gratitude Can Help Us Through Hard Times*

Even when life is not quite how we want it to be, operating from a mood of gratitude will allow us to flow with acceptance, and from that state, we will always live a happier existence. For example, if our current job provides an income, looking at it through the lens of how it is providing for us will help us move into a mood of gratitude. Gratitude is a beautiful mood that helps us experience happiness and joy. It enables us to accept ourselves, accept others and operate from a much calmer way of being. Everything seems possible from gratitude.

3. Wonder – bring back your inner child

Think back to a time when you were a little girl. A time where you didn't have all the answers, and when not knowing didn't bother you. Instead you were **curious**. There was a natural innocence about you. The world appeared to you in all its **wonder**. You were watching and learning with fascination. You had a natural curiosity. You had plenty of questions and you wondered what the answers were.

In this state there were no expectations to be the Good Girl. You felt free. You were open to learn and discover the fascinating big and small things around you. This is the mood of wonder.

Wonder is a mood that can lighten our whole way of being. It shifts the focus away from **doing** and searching for results. It is about **being** in a state of fascination and curiosity. In wonder there is no drive for perfection, there is no room for comparison and overwhelm. Wonder is a mood that enables us to visualise the future and then create possibilities from our visualisation.

Take time to stop and notice the little things

Watch an ant crawling across the concrete pavement carrying food. Where is it going? What is it doing? By honing in on something simple and seeing wonder in it, we are putting all the complications of the world aside. We are training our minds to focus on simplicity with innocent curiosity.

> *Life is not all about the big achievements and big events... it can be about the little things, the simplest but fascinating moments in which we find wonder and joy.*
>
> – Laura

Imagine a time in the past that brought joy and happiness.

It might have been at a beach... or the time you laughed with a friend. Put yourself into the feeling. Close your eyes and stay with it for a minute or two.

When you opened your eyes, what did you notice about your body while you were in that memory? Notice your posture, muscle tension and any sensations you experienced on the inside or outside of your body. Stay with this for about a minute or two.

Every time we choose wonder we give ourselves the opportunity to see the world through a fresh lens – a lens of learning, and of different possibilities. This is the mood of explorers and inventors, change-makers and creators.

– Jeanette

Wonder can develop as a mood when one of our fundamental orientations in life is to accept uncertainty. In wonder we embrace the uncertainty of the world and the mystery of life. We are not preoccupied with the self-protection and seeing the world full of potential harm.

– Alan Sieler, *Coaching to the Human Soul, Ontological Coaching and Deep Change, Volume II*

Wonder is a powerful emotional space that orients us to be a learner.

Wonder and curiosity go hand-in-glove

– Alan Sieler, *Coaching to the Human Soul, Ontological Coaching and Deep Change, Volume II*

When we are experiencing wonder and curiosity, we release the anxiety that comes from striving for perfection, and having to have all the answers. From this mood we will be in a state of fascination and inquiry, always observing greater **possibilities**. Imagine experimenting the path we are on, rather than being stressed that we're not there yet?

Wonder removes the stress response and allows our body to operate at an optimum level.

– Jeanette

Even when we're uncertain about an outcome we can be interested to find out when we see the world through wonder. We're more likely to go about life with lightness and a cheerful attitude of trying new things. This way of being allows us to be okay with making mistakes and learning along the way – this is life's learning curve. It opens us up to many and varied possibilities and it shows us things that may have been invisible to us due to anxiety or fear, shame or embarrassment, anger or resentment.

Below, we share how anxiety, and wonder and curiosity are on opposite sides of the emotional spectrum. When we're experiencing anxiety, it's almost impossible to experience wonder and curiosity. When we're experiencing wonder and curiosity, it's almost impossible to experience anxiety. They have a completely different energy about them.

Anxiety versus Wonder and Curiosity

Overwhelm is a physical condition. Anxiety is a mood that can manifest into the condition of overwhelm.

In the mood of anxiety we're anticipating something may be going to turn out badly and we don't know how we might avoid or deal with it. By living in anxiety we're literally saying to ourselves: *I can't cope with this uncertainty.* We're looking for certainty that the world simply cannot promise us. We make ourselves worry about things we cannot control.

Our body will always struggle to cope when we operate from anxiety. As our mind becomes overloaded with worrying thoughts, we try desperately to figure out how to avoid the worst case scenario.

Imagine we have a project to complete and we're reaching the deadline. We can imagine that we don't finish in time. We can also imagine the people who will be affected by us not meeting the deadline. We might ruminate over a financial fallout. Our reputation might be on the line. Perhaps we made a promise to someone and we don't like breaking promises. We might have a particular standard we set ourselves to reach, and if we can't reach that standard, we may feel as though we've failed. This entire story we write in our minds creates overwhelm. There might be other emotions going on such as frustration, annoyance, fear or doubt. The bottom line here is, in this state, anxiety is the underlying mood which our way of being is operating from.

When we recognise we're in a mood of anxiety we can take notice of what's concerning us, reassess our priorities and commitments and consider how we would like to change things. We can always learn from anxiety. So all is not lost. What anxiety doesn't give us is creativity and belief.

> *Anxiety has an annoying way of tricking us into believing the uncertainties are not worth the risk, and therefore we resist possibilities... On the other hand, wonder and curiosity invites possibilities to dinner and allows the conversations to flow and the creative ideas to come.*
>
> – Jeanette

The thoughts that come out of anxiety, versus curiosity and wonder:

Anxiety says – no way!
Wonder and curiosity says – let's explore!
Anxiety says – I might be damaged!
Wonder and curiosity says – I don't need to know the outcome!

Anxiety says – I must protect myself!
Wonder and curiosity says – **I'm going to give it a go!**
Anxiety says – I don't have the capacity to deal with this!
Wonder and curiosity says – **The world is a fascinating place!**

NOTE: Can you see the Sneaky Declarations in these statements? It's the negative self-talk that has the potential to take us into overwhelm, just like consuming little shots of poison that feed us with doubt about our ability to cope.

How the body reacts:

Anxiety – withdraw and protect
Wonder and curiosity – **wide-eyed and open**
Anxiety – diminishing height
Wonder and curiosity – **chest open**

Can you see how from a mood of anxiety our body supports a negative story?

We're inviting you to observe anxiety through the mood of wonder. Wonder puts us into an optimum learning state, and it's through that state that we will see what anxiety is trying to take care of, then how it isn't serving us for the life we want to create. As we observe our experience of anxiety through this lens, we will begin to learn that wonder has power. Then the more we access wonder, the greater we take on its energy – our way of being in which we predominantly operate from.

Embrace possibilities

Possibilities are everywhere – even when we can't see them. They are right there for us to reach out and explore. Imagining possibilities are around the corner makes us more open to seeing them and accepting them.

How do I want my life to look?

This is a question we can ask through the emotion of wonder. It enables us to visualise the future without worrying about the possible dangers. There is always time to evaluate risks and danger at a later stage once we've explored a whole range of possibilities. Our vision is always more difficult to access and possibilities are more difficult to see when we are predicting danger.

> *When we are living from a mood of wonder, our heart will begin to open to gratitude. And gratitude opens us up to wonder. Overwhelm can't survive when we have wonder, gratitude and simplicity.*

Story – Laura's journey back from burnout

I was exhausted. I was already burnt out when I became a sole parent, so it's not surprising that overwhelm floated around.

In reality, I'd never given myself permission to truly rest. As a parent, I'd dealt continuously with ongoing issues that were affecting my daughters. I couldn't switch off my mind. Everything became an overload.

What helped me recover was self-care and support. I'd lost touch with what that meant. In thinking about everyone else and what I **should** and **shouldn't** be doing, that I'd left myself behind. I saw my lovely doctor who wasn't surprised at my exhaustion. My Auntie came and stayed – I'll never forget that. I didn't feel alone any more. It was when I gave myself permission to stop, rest and catch up on sleep, forgave myself for not being perfect and simplified my life that I began to heal from burnout. After some time something in me shifted. I began to write down what I was grateful for even when I didn't feel like it. I created my own positive declarations – and said them even though I didn't believe them yet. Bit by bit, I recovered.

Now, I can detect early signs of overwhelm before they progress into burnout. Being in a state of overwhelm, as uncomfortable as it feels, lets me know that something in my life needs to change.

> *Overwhelm reminds us to stop being so hard on ourselves, to accept ourselves and to simplify our lives. It can also show us that we need time to be like a child – and experience wonder and gratitude.*

By reducing our physical and mental load as well as understanding our emotional responses to events, we can significantly reduce overwhelm, reduce the stress on our bodies. Rather than seeing overwhelm as a way of living or a way of life, we can see it as a temporary condition that we can shift out of... and expand our inner calm.

POWER ACTION

Practice the mood of wonder

Go and stand outside (with no shoes on if it's not too cold). Preferably stand on the grass, but if you don't have grass, then stand on whatever surface you do have.

Ground yourself: Both feet flat

Knees: Soften your knees

Chest: Lift your chest

Shoulders: Gently make a circle with your shoulders, then let them softly rest

Arms: Hang your arms softly beside your body

Hands: Let them hang loosely by your sides

Face: Soften the muscles in your face

Chin: Lift your chin slightly and look out to the world

Now what do you notice?

What can you see?

What can you hear?

How does the grass feel under your feet?

What things do you find yourself wondering about?

Feel into your body from this way of being. Make a mental or written note of what comes to you. Repeat this each day.

Practice gratitude

Each day for the next week find things in your world that you can be grateful for. As you notice things you can be grateful for, breathe into the experience of gratitude, loosen up your body, look out to the world and see it as a gift. Start the practice of writing down three things you're grateful for at the end of every day.

If we want to start experiencing gratitude we have to start feeling into it rather than waiting for it to come to us. Gratitude is a way of being, not a strategy.

Key Points

- Overwhelm is a sign that your nervous system is telling you it is overloaded
- SIMPLIFY. What's really important – and what's not?
- Gratitude is proven to shift our perspective and overcome overwhelm
- From a mood of wonder and curiosity we can explore how we would like things to be
- Together, simplicity, gratitude and wonder help us overcome overwhelm

Chapter 9

Listen To Your Gut
WHEN THINGS DON'T FEEL RIGHT

The aftermath of Good Girl conditioning

It's our inner guide that suffers through inequality and conditioned people-pleasing. As a result, there's usually a message we are missing that our intuition is insisting on us listening to. The more we continue to ignore these messages, the quieter our inner guide becomes.

When something doesn't feel right but we don't address it, the risk is that we can slip into moods such as anxiety and depression. Especially when our gut is telling us we're ignoring the possibilities of what we might be called to do. The danger of ignoring our gut, is finally getting to the point where we believe we've lost ourselves and our sense of identity.

In the process of feeling as though we are losing a sense of identity we may not observe that we have choices. Imagine a lizard living in a fishbowl... she can see through the glass, but she can't see a way to jump out. She also can't see that there are choices beyond the glass for her.

Years of conditioning can silence that inner voice completely. The good news is, it's not gone forever. We can start to use new practices of listening to our gut and sharpen that inner guide once again.

When something doesn't feel right

Have you ever had a feeling that something doesn't feel right? You know the times you're right in the middle of making a crucial decision and our body is telling you, *no?* Or you're on the cusp of making a decision and your body is telling you, *yes?* These are the moments our gut is trying to tell us that something feels off or something feels right. Our body knows. Our intuition is our inner wisdom.

When your gut is clearly signaling that you should listen. Pause – always pause.

The trouble is, we get so many distractions from the outside world that our inner voice has to fight to be heard. The signal is there – but the outside world and all of its standards and expectations are pulling us into the vortex of constant messages it demands we hear. There's a fight going on and our inner voice is often losing.

That inner knowing

Intuition: *The ability to understand something without needing to think about it or use reason to discover it, or a feeling that shows this ability.*
– Cambridge Dictionary

Intuitive feelings can't necessarily be explained and are often misunderstood. This is really interesting because we use the word **feeling**, to describe our intuition, such as: *I've got a feeling about this.* These feelings can be more powerful than reason and logic but are often missed or not well understood. To understand our intuition we need to realise that the gut and brain interact.

Your gut literally speaks to your brain along something called the gut-brain access. Your gut instinct is real.

– Rebecca Hirst, *How Listening To My Gut Changed Everything*

When Rebecca first decided to study nutrition, she said she knew in her gut that her job was to help busy women and men to feel gloriously well and to feel happy and healthy in their bodies. There was some logical knowing, but the inner knowing – her gut feeling – was the thing that pulled her away from her successful, busy international marketing career to study nutrition. Rebecca said, *You don't just pack up and leave a successful career if you do not have a passion to fill and the inner knowing that this is the right path for you.*

If we don't listen to our gut feeling, there is a risk we will miss the clues it's sending us. We rely so heavily on reason that our gut often doesn't get a voice. While our thinking-brain is designed to help us plan, prepare, make daily decisions and develop crucial skills and knowledge, as well as apply that knowledge, it does not give us the ability to sense and to feel.

> *Our intuition is there to guide us and illuminate our inner knowing. We can use it to tune into the things that are important to us that will lead us to the pathways we'd like to take.*

Gut and emotions

Gut feeling can also be preceded or followed by emotions. Our emotions bring on body sensations such as a knot in our stomach, a sudden warm feeling, a tingling in our arms or legs or a tightness in our chest. This is our body trying to send us messages. If we take the time to work out what it's trying to tell us, we will get a much clearer picture than if we just relied on logic.

To open ourselves up to the inner knowing our gut feelings bring us, we can tune in and say: *Ah yes, there you are! What are you trying to tell me?* This process is a deeper listening to the concerns which reveal themselves to us by feelings and body sensations, muscle tension, posture, voice tone, and volume.

Every choice we make has an emotional element to it, but we have been mislead about our emotions. We have been lead to believe that logic and rationale is much more reliable. Yet at our core we are emotion-**ing** beings. To strengthen our gut feeling, emotions must always be involved.

You've got this and your gut knows it!

The Silent Pause

Taking a pause gives us time to listen to the voice that may have been silenced. The pause gives us time to think about what concerns us, regroup and get clear about which way we'd like to proceed. It also gives us the ability to tune into our emotional experiences, which will help us see what's missing in our lives.

Pausing gives us time to look at:
- What's going on for us – our perceptions and interpretations
- What's going on for others – their perceptions and interpretations
- What really concerns us
- What really concerns others

We can't possibly know what others are thinking and feeling in the absence of conversations and even then, they may not share everything. Without a conversation, we will come to conclusions by drawing from our own interpretations. The silent pause can give us the space to think about the important things we want to consider – and possible conversations we may want to have.

POWER ACTION
Mindfulness Breathing Awareness

Do some exercise for about 20 minutes or so – go for a walk, cycle, swim, yoga, Tai Chi or anything that helps to calm your nervous system and reset your emotions.

Now find a place to sit with your back upright, either in a chair or on the floor, with your back supported. Allow yourself to close your eyes and sit quietly for at least five minutes. Become aware of your body. Allow yourself to focus your attention on your breathing, and just simply be aware.

You may have a tendency to **judge** how well you are breathing, but this exercise is not about breathing techniques. It is about simply observing and noting your breathing no matter how it's happening.

You will probably find your attention wandering onto other things, such as the various thoughts about what is going on in your world. This is quite natural. Simply observe what happens in your attention and gently refocus it on your breathing.

Now see what you notice as you go about your day. Are you more in tune with your body and your gut feelings?

Repeating this practice a few times a week will help you become more aware of your intuitive powers – and your gut feelings.

Key Points

- Your gut speaks to you along the gut-brain access
- Your gut instinct is real
- When your gut is signalling to you, pause
- When there's a fight going on between the outside world and your gut, listen to your gut
- We rely so heavily on reason – our gut rarely gets a listen
- Our thinking brain doesn't give us the chance to think and feel
- Listen to your emotions and your gut feeling, as well as reason and logic and use this combination to inform your decisions

Chapter 10

The Power of Your Words

FINDING YOUR VOICE

Words first and the world follows.
– Alan Sieler Newfield Institute

Be quiet. Stop being so sensitive. You're being silly. Sound like familiar messages?

If we did receive these messages as a little girl or a grown woman, what did it tell us? That our voice was an intrusion? That our thoughts weren't valid or important? That we were too loud or boisterous or naughty? That our emotions weren't reasonable. Or that words of people with more power carried more weight and authority?

This message can have us doubting our value and the importance and power of our words and our ability to convey a message. It can leave us finding it hard to trust our decisions, know what our concerns are and then express them clearly.

Years of this conditioning to be quiet or being dismissed can have **us** holding the belief that we're not worthy enough or that our point of view is not valid. It's possible this may have resulted in us shrinking, fading into the background or others having authority over us.

Story – When they wouldn't listen

Have you ever had the experience of not being taken seriously?

I expressed my deep concerns about one of my children. Every time I reached out, my words were minimised, dismissed or simply not quite understood. I didn't downplay the situation. Instead, I used strong and factual words to describe what had been happening over a long length of time. No matter what I said or how I said it, it didn't give weight to my words.

I felt deflated, frustrated and invalidated.

One day I received a message from someone in a position of authority who had been in contact with my child. This person stated they saw a **major** concern. That one word mirrored what I had tried to explain. There were moments where I had questioned myself. This validation told me I could and should have trusted my thoughts and the words I used to express myself, in the first place.

– Laura

Giving ourselves authority to believe in our own voice opposes the inaccurate story that others are better, stronger, and have a right to share their knowledge, skills and wisdom **more so** than we do. With a new self-authoring story, we are not only powerful, but we give ourselves the right to have a voice with grace, dignity and confidence.

Just like the Suffragettes who stood up against inequality with their voices, we too have that right. What we have to say and what we have to offer the world matters.

> I am a smart, capable and courageous *woman*

Story – Two little boys

The day I learned those two little boys at the swim school were obviously living with domestic violence I stated, *This is horrendous. This has to change. Something has to be done about this.*

What I felt that day affected me down to my soul. What I didn't realise at the time was that the words and the way I felt would become the manifestation of what I would do years later.

It was as though I had all of a sudden pulled my rose-coloured glasses off. As my innocent fifteen year old self, I observed the world through a new murky and troublesome lens that I believed I would someday, somehow be responsible for changing. I had no idea how, but my words on that day changed my future.

I left it far longer than I would have liked. This was because my childhood experiences taught me it wasn't okay to have a voice. Today things have changed. I do have a voice and I have a platform to speak about what truly matters to me. I created a different reality so that other women could do the same, and by doing so, they could have a voice, and positively influence their sons, daughters and someday grandchildren.

– Jeanette

Your silent voice – the words in your mind on autopilot

You know that little voice in your head that just doesn't stop? It's constantly running on autopilot. It reminds you of who you are, who you have come to be and who you think you should be. This is where your harshest self-judgments are. This is the voice that is shaped by your past.

The trouble is, we rarely hear this voice. It's this voice that repeatedly plays in the background until we become aware of it and observe how it is impacting our lives. It's the voice that largely goes unnoticed.

The silent voice is the constant voice of concern. It echoes our experiences and the things we're pondering or worried about. It's like a constant processor, trying to figure out how to handle situations and work out the next move to make. If you listen, it will come across louder than you realise. Sometimes it will come to you as a gut feeling. *(Refer to the previous chapter)*

Your loud voice – the words we speak

These are the words we say out loud to ourselves and to others.

When we're concerned about something, we get a laser-sharp focus on it. These reflect the things that truly matter to us and the things that haven't yet been taken care of, such as finances, career, support, family, transport and our future aspirations.

Sharing various parts of our concerns with others can help us get them off our chests and make sense of them. Our loud voice may have been silent for a while... waiting to be heard and to be given a voice. Both the silent voice and the loud voice can hold powerful statements which change the future.

We call these **declarations**.

Declarations (how we change our future)

Declarations are a statement about **what will be from this time on.**

> *Words first and then the world.*
> – Alan Sieler

What Alan means here is that by declaring something we change our future reality, and that comes about through speaking and listening. Even if we don't like or agree with what we're declaring, there is potential for it to become our reality just through the act of declaring.

Core Beliefs are declarations we fundamentally label ourselves as.

Examples of Core Beliefs:
I'm not smart.
I'm stupid.
I'm shy.
I'm not lovable.
I'm not deserving.
I don't belong.
I'm not enough.

Beliefs about what we are unable to do are also **declarations**.
Examples:
I can't play basketball.
I'm not very good at picking partners.
I don't use public transport because I'm scared I'll get lost.
I'm never going to drive again.
I don't know how to cook.
I'm struggling to know who I am.
It's really hard to make ends meet.
I'm hopeless at managing money.
I'm never going to find someone who loves me.

When we declare these things, we are creating the future for ourselves. The trick is to catch ourselves so we can circumvent the negative beliefs and turn them into positive beliefs.

There is a trap to declarations – there are many silent declarations that go unnoticed at least until something stops us in our tracks and tells us to finally pay attention.

Sneaky Declarations are ones we don't hear in our silent or loud voice.

They can be quite critical. When something goes wrong in our life and we're struggling to figure out how to manage it, we can be very quick to make negative self-judgment.

When we're struggling to pay the rent we might say something like: *I have no money, so I can't meet the house payment or rent this week.* Underneath that concern might be a Sneaky Declaration such as: *I am hopeless at managing money.*

If we're looking for a partner we might say something like: *I can't get a partner. All my dates have been flops. No one will want to be with me.* Underneath that could be the belief: *I am not lovable.*

The examples we have given above are negative Sneaky Declarations – but Sneaky Declarations can be positive too. Without realising it, we are living out our beliefs through the words we use, and the emotions we experience.

The brain does not know the difference between what's real and what's an illusion...

What's interesting is: When we declare what we don't want, we'll get it, and when we declare what we do want, we'll get it. When we declare who we are at our core, we will come to believe it. The more we focus on and speak about the negative, the stronger our negative beliefs about ourselves become. When that happens there is very little space for change.

Having these negative thoughts about ourselves is one part of the problem, and the fact that they can go so unnoticed is the second part of the problem. The more we catch ourselves saying them, the greater the observer we will become and the greater our chances to change what we've come to believe.

Positive Declarations

We have to consistently make powerful declarations to create the reality we want. However, for positive declarations to stick and create permanent change, they have to be made from an elevated emotion. If we want something to be different, the emotion or mood we experience it from has to change too.

Speaking with strength

Including words in our speech such as **just, I think**, or **only** will modify the meaning we are trying to convey. This can be very disempowering, especially when we're wanting to share a strong point, an opinion or make a request. It's common for girls and women in particular to use these words to soften what they are saying or asking for.

Two examples:
I'm just an admin person.
Instead of: *I work in admin.*
I'm just contacting you because I'm wondering if you'd be able to help me.
Instead of: *Can you please assist me?*

Words are so powerful. They declare our future. The strength of our words matter.

I invest in me every single day because I am worth it

Ditching other people's opinions of us

The truth is we all have opinions. But there is a risk of treating other people's opinions as the truth, when they're clearly an **opinion**. As soon as the words leave someone's mouth they are given a life. When we take them on as though they're the truth, we give them a longer life.

All opinions we take on, negative or positive, shape what we believe about ourselves. They influence the actions we take – or don't take. We give them the power to place limitations on us. Even when they're outdated or inaccurate we may still take them on as though they are a part of us if we allow it to happen.

They may not necessarily sound negative and that's why they're so sneaky. They can simply be statements that define who others think we are, or statements about what they want us to be. They can be labels that put us in boxes that shut down possibilities if we take them on, or allow others to force them on us.

There is as much danger in taking on people's positive opinions as there is taking on the negative opinions. Sometimes it's nice to have external encouragement, but when we have a pattern of depending on that validation in order to feel worthy, there's a risk of us not trusting our own inner validation. Either way, we get to decide what we take on and what we don't.

We might have heard declarations like:
You're stupid.
You're always late.
Women are manipulative.
Women are the carers and nurturers.
You're such a good mum.
You're so beautiful.

> *We have to think it and speak it before it becomes what we want it to be.*
>
> – Jeanette

Our brains can turn things around

Positive declarations are incredibly powerful. Our brain has a clever way of believing everything we tell it. Even if what we're saying or believing is an illusion, it can be taken on as though it's the truth. In this case, it's important to not take on negative declarations, but it's equally as important to turn negative declarations into positive declarations... then repeat them enough times for our brain to believe them.

Whatever belief we want to hold about ourselves is our choice. We can challenge all of the old and outdated beliefs that we hold about ourselves and declare new ones. But there's one thing we have to do first. Since deep down we believe these negative things about ourselves, we have to get really clear about what **is** and what **isn't** a fact.

Facts versus assessments (judgements and opinions)

There's something revealing about all of a sudden realising our judgements and opinions are not the truth. Humans throw opinions around... and they multiply and become misconstrued.

There's a very easy way to distinguish between what is actually factual and what isn't.

For example:
1. We have a situation: the car broke down.
2. We have our thoughts about the car breaking down, such as: *I'll be late for work. The boss will be angry. I won't get my project completed. Everyone will think I'm lazy. I am lazy.*

The FACT:
The car broke down

The ASSESSMENTS:
I'll be late for work (could be substantiated).
The boss will be angry (could be substantiated).
I won't get my project completed.
Everyone will think I'm lazy.
I am lazy.

Facts can only be substantiated when there's evidence.

If the boss has been angry when we've been late in the past, then this could be considered to be factual. If the car can't be fixed quickly, then being late for work could be substantiated, but it is harder to substantiate the remaining opinions. **However, by stating these beliefs we can bring them into existence. This would be Sneaky Declarations in action.**

> *Honestly, if you ask me, facts and opinions are constantly competing in the ring – and no one is winning!*
>
> – Jeanette

In the case of mistreatment, some people use words as weapons to hurt others. They wield words that are completely untrue to make up stories about the person they are seeking to abuse. They may name call or treat the person as though they are not worthy or smart. Hurtful and damaging words are stated with such conviction to try and convince the target that the negative opinions about them are true.

Words being used against us can prompt us to doubt our own thoughts and our own reality. It can also have us questioning our emotions. It's when we believe toxic, untrue words are the truth that they become part of who we think we are. This can leave us feeling flattened, vulnerable and weak.

It is our right to question the validity of any assessments made about us. There is no basis for negative assessments. They will never serve us for what we want to create in our lives, and **we** have the right to decide how to listen to them in the future.

> *As humans, we have a social responsibility to choose our words wisely instead of tossing them around like crap on a wall and ignoring the effect they have on those we choose to target.*
>
> – Jeanette

Words from Jeanette

People make assessments all the time. My mentor Alan Sieler says, **We are assessment making machines.**

I personally hear ungrounded assessments everyday. We **all** make them. None of us are immune from being assessment making machines.

It's the judgements sitting behind the assessments that bother me the most – the judgements that we are somehow not living up to someone else's standards, or that our values don't align with theirs.

It shocks and challenges our personal values and biases when people fail to demonstrate behaviour we find acceptable. People are often attached to being right. We regularly see this in various sides of politics – politicians fight and argue, rarely demonstrating to the public they are capable of collaboration across parties, or even within their own party. This attitude filters down through the fabric of society. They are our leaders and many of them are showing a poor example.

When we see the judgements and opinions for what they are, we can reject them. By doing that, we open up different possibilities for ourselves.

Our reality will change when we become a more powerful observer of our words and the words of others around us. From these powerful new ways of observing we can declare powerful statements for ourselves. Then we can truly know beyond a shadow of a doubt that we are valuable human beings.

> *By creating our own declarations, we are actively choosing and writing our own future story.*

POWER ACTION
Observing Assessments

Being a more intuitive observer of assessments which have become Sneaky Declarations is a powerful everyday practice.

Become a powerful creator of your own future

1. Observe

First, think about something in your life that isn't going as well as you'd like it to, something you'd want to make a change to. Write that down in as much detail as you want to in a couple of paragraphs. Take about 10 minutes or so. No need to filter it – no one else is going to see it.

Once you've done this, read through it and write down all the assessments (judgements and opinions) that:

1. come to you in your silent voice
2. you read in the words on the page

No need to change what you have written or picked up in your silent voice. This is all about observing. This is an exercise to help you observe the sneaky assessments and declarations in breakdowns.

2. Declare what you want

Now create one positive declaration about yourself – about the future self you'd like to be.

Examples:
> *I am peaceful, strong and calm.*
> *I'm good at doing hard things.*
> *I'm becoming more organised every day.*

Well done! You're now starting to be a different observer and a creator of your own reality.

Instead of worrying and having anxiety about what may happen next, we can practice thinking of the future as an interesting adventure. What exciting possibilities could be around the corner?

– Jeanette and Laura

Key Points

- Declarations are powerful statements that shape your reality
- Sneaky Declarations are those that are currently invisible
- We don't have to accept other peoples' assessments of us
- Assessments are judgements and opinions
- We are assessment making machines

Chapter 11

Set Clear Boundaries

FREEDOM FROM CONTROL

The aftermath of living in a world where girls have been told who they should be means we can lose sight of who we are, what *we* want and how we want to be treated.

We have the right to ask for what we want and say no to what we don't want. But why is this so hard sometimes? Maybe it's because we've tiptoed gently around difficult conversations for so long. Maybe it's also because we've never really believed we have a right to truly be our own authority.

Knowing how to set boundaries and ask for things that are important to us is not just a skill, it's a way of being.

We have to be able to know what we want, know we have a right to ask for it, then make requests in the right mood *(more on the power of moods further down)*. Asking for what we want and setting clear boundaries can be part of the same conversation.

Story – The woman who picked up the slack

Every day at work Jenny* found herself picking up the slack from some other colleagues. Some of the other women at work had been given higher paid roles. Jenny felt this was unfair but continued to work hard at compensating for their more ultra-relaxed approach to work.

During coaching Jenny realised she was in the habit of being everything to everyone. This meant she would do things asked of her without question. She would even do extra work that no one asked her to do, simply because she could see it needed doing. It also meant that Jenny didn't know how to ask for what she needed and wanted. She was becoming resentful and despondent. She was losing motivation at work and wondered what she could do about it – after all, she held herself to high standards.

Three things had to happen for Jenny to once again be happy and motivated at work. She planned to change the situation by:
1. Asking for support from colleagues
2. Putting boundaries in place for herself so she wasn't tempted to do everything all the time
3. Asking if the organisation would support her to do further study to qualify for a higher paid role

* name changed

Being everything to everyone often means we have poor boundaries. A woman who has been everything to everyone else her whole life doesn't know how to set boundaries. It's not until circumstances nearly break her that she may finally realise that if she doesn't set boundaries, she will continue to suffer.

Setting boundaries can include:
- Being sure about what we won't do
- Being sure about what we will do
- Giving ourselves the physical space we want
- Making requests – having important conversations

Our mood sets the tone

Humans are not only linguistic beings, constituted in language, they are also emotional beings. To be human is to live in a continual flow of moods and emotions, like a 'stream of feeling', that is intertwined with our desires and preferences, and what matters to us.

– Alan Sieler, Newfield Institute, *Coaching to the Human Soul Ontological Coaching and Deep Change Volume II*

We can't step into our conversations without a mood. Because we're always taking actions through emotions, we are emotion-**ing** beings. Therefore, our moods shape the tone and nature of the conversation.

Not being clear on our boundaries or having poor boundaries can result in us carrying a mood of resentment. It can also result in resignation that nothing we do will make a difference. Carrying moods of resentment and resignation that nothing will make a difference no matter what we ask for, will not change the outcome. If we're not getting what we want, or we're getting things we don't want, we have to look at the mood we are taking action from.

Our moods change the tone of our voice. They also affect our posture – and our posture affects our mood. Therefore, moods and posture also affect our ability to have courageous conversations. Courage is a strong and powerful mood. It doesn't resent, it doesn't get angry. It just stays strong and supports us to ask for what we want.

Imagine walking into a room of employees to ask for support in a mood of **anxiety**, or **resentment**. The conversation would be quite different than if our mood was **ambition**, **curiosity** or **acceptance**.

Notice the different tones people use when they speak. Have you noticed that people who sound less sure or who speak with less confidence end their sentences on a higher note? Strong leaders tend to speak firmly in a low tone. They don't usually waver in their speech. The tone they use is rarely high. What mood do you think a strong leader may have when she or he speaks?

Standing strong in our boundaries

Good Girls find it hard to put up boundaries because they believe they should always think about what everyone else wants and how everyone else feels.

This is a very bold statement that's not necessarily true for all of us, but it's worth thinking about in the context of what it means to be a Good Girl. We can take notice of how we respond to people's needs and what other people ask from us.

Do we need more boundaries? We can ask ourselves:
- *When someone makes a demand do we always respond with a yes?*
- *When someone commands our time do we ignore our need for space?*
- *When someone criticises us do we allow them to do it?*
- *When someone tells us what we **should** do, do we comply?*
- *When someone behaves badly, do we apologise for speaking up about it?*

How important is it to command respect and be treated with dignity? When we set boundaries, it's important to keep the values of respect and dignity at the forefront of our minds. When we command dignity and respect, the outcome of the conversation will be very different. Dignity and respect does not require us to act out of anger, resentment or frustration. These are all lower energy moods that don't support positive interactions or outcomes.

Now, the more I realise my qualities are a strength, the less I am inclined to give them away to somebody too quickly.

– Meredith, You Vitality

We have a right to stand our ground and live by our values, so we can choose to have the conversations that are important to us. Boundary setting can be done in a respectful and dignified way.

Is it service or sacrifice?

The narrative: **women have to be everything to everyone else** means dropping everything we're doing to help someone else who needs our time and support. It's not their request that makes us do what they want us to do. It's our willingness to fulfill their request and the validation we get from that, which can be an addiction that keeps us coming back for more.

For a woman who is conditioned to be everything to everyone else, it's easy to jump at the whiff of a perceived need. **Yes** can be our automatic response. Always saying **yes** is a recipe for exhaustion and frustration.

In that process we can consider if what we are about to do feels like service or sacrifice. It might just be as simple as finding a balance.

So what is the difference between service and sacrifice?

Sacrifice is when we do something for others in a way that depletes us. **Service** is when we do something for others in a way that supports or nurtures us both. No one can tell us whether we are in service or sacrifice. Only we know the difference. Knowing the difference means tuning inward to see how it feels.

We can do this by pausing. Firstly, the pause will allow us to identify the sense of urgency we many feel inside – that habitual pull to jump in and give of ourselves. Or it will help us to recognise genuine joy we feel at the thought of supporting. Secondly, pausing gives us the space to take stock and consider our own needs. Pausing then empowers us to choose our response and set the conditions around the support we are willing to provide.

Pausing not only allows us to observe how we manage our commitments... it also empowers us to question whether our everyday responses are tied into our identity as a woman, and whether in this narrative, we are sacrificing more than is healthy for us.

> *'I'll think about it and get back to you', gives us time to pause and think about how we want to respond.*

Quick tips to pause with power

We can ask ourselves right before we respond:
1. Am I **perceiving** that I'm needed?
2. Will doing this give me validation?
3. Am I feeling a sense of urgency – a compulsion that I must act immediately?
4. If yes, is the situation **truly urgent**?
5. Has there been a clear request or is it a demand?
6. How would I like to respond?

Pausing and thinking about whether we're in service or sacrifice gives us a bit more time to think about the things we're committing to.

Examples of when we perceive we are needed:
- We jump to help clients who ask for more than the agreed commitment
- We offer not to charge people for our services
- We always let in friends and family members who show up at our doorstep, no matter what – and cancel our plans
- We neglect our own needs and instead respond quickly to friends and family members who text or call us with problems

Sometimes we feel we have to respond straight away when there is no legitimate urgency... but that doesn't mean we have to.

Is a building on fire? Is there a child missing? Does someone need an ambulance?

Sometimes people just need to learn to wait – and many people will wait as long as we're respectfully clear. It doesn't mean we have to explain our commitments... we just need to state what we are and aren't willing to do. The more we jump, the more people expect of us and that's not their fault.

Responding to requests

Brene Brown, Researcher Professor, refers to responding to the wants of others when she says, *Choose discomfort over resentment.*

> *Discomfort allows us to have better conversations. We can feel the discomfort, choose the conversation and our mood – then take action.*

Every single day of our lives we are either responding to requests or making requests. This is how we get things done, coordinate action and take care of things that truly matter to us. If we didn't make requests, society would not progress.

Think about these institutions and individuals within them, such as children, teachers, CEO's, managers, customers and parents:
- Families
- Schools
- Businesses
- Organisations
- Political parties
- Media

Everything achieved in all of these institutions and groups of people is done through making requests, making promises and making offers to get things done.

Unfortunately many requests are ineffective. Very often they are more like demands or pleas. A demand or a plea doesn't give people the opportunity to consider their response. So many requests are left unfulfilled because the mood the request was made in was not congruent with respect and dignity. Demands and pleas directed at us can leave us feeling as though we have no choice but to respond with **yes.**

Many of us feel as though we are run off our feet. Not only do we not know how to effectively respond to requests, but we don't know how to ask them of other people. This is a major contributor to having poor boundaries.

Alan Sieler says there are four ways (plus one) we can respond to requests:
1. **Accept** – yes, we'll do it
2. **Decline** – no, we won't do it

3. **Counter-offer** – we offer up a counter offer we are happy with
4. **Commit-to-commit later** – get back to them at an agreed date or time with a decision

And then there's what Alan calls the **Slippery Promise!**

This means we say in the moment that we'll do something, but we don't take the time to pause and think our response through or intend to actually do what we have committed to. Things may never get done with a Slippery Promise.

Making clear requests

We make requests because as humans we work together, live together and in the process of life are dependent on others.

People ask requests in four different ways:

Unclear request – and without important details
Clear request – with the conditions and details laid out clearly
Demand – insisting we do it or else
Plea – *pleasssssseeeeee can you do this for me?*

When we make a request in frustration that we're not being listened to – or in resignation that nothing will change, our request is likely to come across as a plea. Demanding or pleading doesn't give people the appropriate time to respond. Asking in a rush in the heat of the moment is unlikely to give people the time they need to digest our request.

On the other hand, when we are calm and clear, we are more likely to get our message across. Then people can decide on their response.

We can learn how to make effective requests by choosing to do the following...
- Choose a resourceful mood
- Be clear about what we're asking for
- Be specific about what we're asking for
- Let others know why it is important to us

- Give a time frame for the request to be completed
- Make sure the mood of the other person is conducive to listening

Moods are often overlooked in the request-making process. If we make requests from moods such as anxiety, fear or resignation, it is more likely it will come across as a demand. It is less likely that we will be heard and responded to in the way we expect.

We can't always be certain that our requests will be fulfilled, particularly if we're asking someone to perform a new skill. Many trainees don't fulfill requests because they're nervous or uncertain about what's being asked of them. When we're setting a new expectation, we might need to teach more than once, modify our request according to the person's skills, break down the components and clarify more than once.

For example, when we ask a child to clean their bedroom we have to make sure our request is age appropriate and gives the child opportunity to scaffold their skills. It's pointless asking a two-year-old to make their bed, put everything away in the correct boxes and vacuum the floor.

Some requests are simple and we can respond to them straight away without too much thought. Such as: *Would you mind making me a cup of tea?* Some are more complicated and need more thought.

> *Some people say they listen to around 50 requests a day or maybe more. Imagine how this turns out when so many of our requests are ineffective?*

Dealing with authoritarian demands

Some people come across as authoritarians. They believe it is their right to control us and tell us what we should do and how we should think. They demand obedience and often oppose our freedom to think and decide for ourselves.

An authoritarian person often displays aggressive behaviour. They can come across as intelligent and sound very persuasive. They act as though they are the superior holders of the truth.

*An **authoritarian** leader is aggressive, lacks empathy, cares only about their own needs and also has a very low tolerance for frustration. They're incapable of seeing the needs of others. Moreover, they often act against them because they view them as weaknesses.* **Authoritarian people cast a long, menacing shadow over our lives.** *Whether in the family, at work, or in politics, you know it when you see it, by their use and abuse of power. In their minds you'll find prejudice and a need to dominate, as well as cynicism, double standards and intolerance.*

– 7 Characteristics of Authoritarian People, According to Psychology, exploringyourmind.com

Their expectations are beyond what is reasonable and yet their overconfident demeanour and aggressiveness has the potential to cause us to doubt ourselves and lose confidence. They are often telling us what we **should** do and who we **should** be. Usually this is preceded with their unreasonable standard. Very little we do is right in the eyes of an authoritarian. They have a double standard. They have a set of rules for us – but rules don't apply to them.

Authoritarians don't necessarily come across as authoritarian all the time. They can be charming and have other positive traits. This helps them blend in, so it can be difficult to identify them. When they make a promise, it may seem that they're trying to take care of us. However, it could be part of their attempt to control us.

An authoritarian may say: *I promise this will never happen to you again... not on my watch*. While this may sound caring and protective, underneath their words may be sneaky words that serve to control.

A person who has authoritarian traits may be judging us because they believe they have the authority to put us in our place. Watch out for the language of obligation in the words they use when they speak to us.

Examples:
You can't do that.
You should do this.

When authoritarians don't like our response to their demands

People who are demanding typically don't respect other people's boundaries. There's a good chance they will react negatively when we don't comply to their demands. Angry words may spill out of their mouths. We can't control that. We can't stop people reacting negatively but we can choose our response to their reactions. We can decide how we receive them and create our future boundaries in response to their reactions.

Authoritarians are also experts at emotional manipulation, with the attempt to enforce guilt when we don't comply.

> *Authoritarians make demands but we have the right to be the authority in our own lives and we don't have to submit to any demands that come our way.*

A demand is not a request. With a demand, we are not given the **choice** of a response. There is an expectation that we will say yes. A demand is an attempt by someone else to ensure their needs will be met.

We all need a boundary audit from time to time

We're human after all.

It's never too late to reassess what we do and don't want in our lives. It's also never too late to put clear boundaries in place and make clear requests. Saying no to others is saying yes to ourselves. We are responsible for our own boundaries.

Setting boundaries is about recognising our own values and then setting our own standards and expectations around those values. It's also about making sure we are not living to fulfill other people's standards and expectations and do what that they insist we should do. People are not going to thank us at the end of our lives for having no boundaries and letting them walk all over us.

Each of us is stronger and more capable than we think. If we haven't set clear boundaries in the past, we can learn to put them in place now.

A boundary audit means assessing whether our own boundaries are in place and if they're not, what we would like to do about that. Once again, this comes back to tuning into that gut feeling. If something feels icky it probably is. Remember that our body is our wisdom. Having tuned into our wisdom gives us the insight to determine what boundaries need to be set.

Story – No is a complete sentence

I remember when I received a particularly persuasive, authoritarian email. The person writing to me was insisting that I should take a particular action. Everything sounded convincing... and there was a sense of urgency in the email to do as they were telling me to do. Something wasn't sitting right with me. I wanted to come up with a respectful and yet firm way to say no, however, I sensed they would be angry and unhappy with my decline. I believed I needed to come up with solid reasons as to why I was declining their demand. I asked a friend if she had any tips on this.

*I know **exactly** how you can say no*, she said.

Oh yes, please tell me, I replied, waiting for her articulate suggestion.

*You just say **no. No**. Nothing else is needed.*

But, I said.

She responded with, *No. **Just NO**. You don't need to explain yourself. And the moment you give reasons, you are giving the person the opportunity to argue with your reasons. No is **no**. And **no** is a complete sentence.*

*Wow. I can just say no? NOTHING ELSE? Just **no**?* This profound and yet ultra simple knowledge liberated me. Why on earth didn't I think of that earlier?

On reflection, previously spending time constructing thoughtful and thorough responses to this person had not worked previously. And my time had not been appreciated. It was in my power to claim my time back and give myself the freedom to respond with an ultra simple, one-word boundary: *No.* That day I found my **no** – and I was determined to never lose it again.

– Laura

Key Points

- It's not our role to be responsible for what others want
- Pausing gives us time to think clearly and respond to the requests and demands of others
- Authoritarians make demands but **we** are the authority of our lives
- Watch out for the language of **obligation**
- Responses to requests: yes, no, counter offer or commit-to-commit later
- Before making a request, choose a resourceful mood that you will make the request from – such as acceptance, ambition or curiosity
- When making a request, be clear and specifically state why it's important to you
- Request and negotiate a timeframe for the request to be completed

POWER ACTION

Game: I'm the queen of my castle

Think of yourself as the queen of your castle

- Stand tall, up high in your castle
- Look beyond the walls with confidence
- Notice the moat outside the walls

- It is a thick moat that surrounds the grounds of the castl
- Feel the energy coming from the water of your moa
- This energy is your invisible shield
- It shields everything outside of the castle
- It affords you time and choice
- As queen of your castle... you are the authority!
- You always have the power of time
- You always have the power of choice
- You always have the power of response
- You always have the power to make the next move
- Your moat protects you from absorbing someone else's words
- You can reject them, turn them back, or let them in
There are two conditions for letting them in:
- They don't tell you what to do
- They don't tell you how to behave

If they break these conditions you get to choose your next move.

Remember as you stand there looking out across the water of your moat, that many of these people care about you. Knowing this allows you to be in your castle with gratitude and appreciation.

The people who you sense care more about what's important to **them** are people you can still look upon with gratitude – they came into your life to teach you just how strong and powerful you are.

Chapter 12

Spring-Clean Your Friends List
CHOOSE YOUR CHEERLEADERS

Detoxing from Good Girl Syndrome can involve assessing who is in our lives... and deciding who we want to spend more of our time with.

It also means recognising unhealthy behaviour and reducing our exposure to people who behave in unhealthy ways around us. It's deciding to be treated with respect and dignity. And spending our time with people who bring out the best in us. It's when we spend time with people who are positive and uplifting that we can concentrate on fulfilling our potential. Cheerleaders can be existing friends and family or new friends.

When people say and do hurtful things to us, it can mean they are projecting what's inside them onto us. When we're being judged, we can find ourselves struggling to validate our views and our worth. It can seem like a battle of views and opinions, rather than being each other's greatest supporters.

We have an important choice to make about the quality of interactions and relationships we want to have. Standing in our own authority, having courageous conversations and maintaining our dignity is a **positive** challenge we face when choosing our cheerleaders.

We need to be clear about what it means to be a good friend, and what we want our community to look and feel like. In a community that is respectful, accepting and supportive, we will thrive.

> *It is both our sanctuary and our destiny to live a life with love, belonging, connection and community.*
>
> – Kon Karapanagiotidis, Founder of the Asylum Seeker Resource Centre

What is a friend?

Good friends don't tell us how things should be and they don't tell us how things are. They don't make up negative stories about us or other people around us, and they don't try to take our sense of control away. They allow us to be unapologetically who we are and they respect our choices and wishes. If we can't be with them, they don't judge, they understand.

A friend is one who encourages our passions and pursuits, refrains from judging our mistakes, accepts us for who we are and loves us unconditionally. A friend listens, empathises and provides a listening ear and comfort when times are tough. A friend expects us to take responsibility for our own actions and yet they don't try and tell us how we should live. They treat us as though the answers are already within us – a friend knows **we've got this**. A friend is respectful and cheers us on. Friends bring us joy, make us laugh, and fire us up to be the best version of ourselves. They also remind us that we're enough just as we are.

The more we observe what it means to be a good friend, the more we realise what we don't want in a friend. When we're clear on this, we will be able to treasure the special people in our lives and celebrate the uniqueness we each bring to our relationships. We will also be more receptive to opening our minds and reaching out to new people.

Giving time to people who enrich our lives and who enrich the lives of others means having a village that provides a buffer from the storms of life. These supportive communities bring us connection, meaning, happiness and belonging.

We are wired for connection. No one is meant to live or struggle alone.

> *Notice how our body and mind feels when we are with friends who treat us as equals. They are the ones who are open and respectfully honest, who embrace our quirks and laugh with us. They are the ones who make life seem easier... and show us we are not alone.*
>
> – Laura

Story – finding my people

Moving house meant making new friends. My daughters climbed the fence and chatted to the kids next door. Before long they all played together like cousins. *Are we having dinner with the neighbours?* is the question all our kids have asked since.

We've celebrated birthdays together on picnics or played in beautiful Warrandyte River. Our kids ran wild together with rocks, mud and several overly ecstatic dogs. When I wasn't well, I've had flowers and a magazine left as a surprise at my door and even a hearty casserole for tea. The kids next door would come over after school if their parents were working late. Our kids would climb into each others' yards to play. It was disappointing when they had to move, but they're not too far away.

We've had a couple and their baby move in next door. Now we are lucky to also call them dear friends. We also have other families we call friends who live close by. This has greatly enriched our lives. We are there for each other. All of us as adults have empathised with each other over hardships. We've brainstormed ideas and celebrated our little successes and funny moments.

– Laura

When should we rethink our friends?

> *You are the average of the five people you spend the most time with.*
>
> – Jim Rohn

Re-thinking our friends can be an uncomfortable topic. Especially if we have been loyal and we value every single person for the part they have played in our lives.

There's a certain level of vulnerability that comes about through no longer accepting our environment as it is. In this vulnerability we find the motivation to change because all of a sudden we can see what we don't like and we can start to imagine how we want things to be.

When we're in the midst of change, it can feel very unsettling. While the familiar may feel safe and comfortable, this might not serve us in the long term. The process we go through when we're finding new ways to be with ourselves also means finding new ways to be with our existing friends, or choosing new friends. No matter how uncomfortable it feels, the discomfort can be a necessary tunnel of time.

We will always know innately when a friendship doesn't feel quite right. We will have a sense of the energy we absorb when we're around different people. If we're feeling a sense of lightness after spending time with someone, then it's probably good for us. On the other hand, if we consistently feel controlled, heavy or weighed down when we're around them, we need to ask ourselves why.

How do we know when a friendship has become toxic?
- We feel guilty for not meeting their expectations
- They consistently dominate conversations
- There is an unequal power balance in conversations
- They're consistently negative or judgemental of us or others
- They consistently interrupt us
- They are disrespectful of us or others
- They talk negatively about us behind our backs
- They're not open to give and take

There are times in our lives when we need to say goodbye and walk away.

When friends don't like our change

Sometimes our personal change can feel very disruptive to our friends. They can become challenged by our change and frightened that they might lose the version of us they have always known and been comfortable with. They may also perceive our change as a threat that we're pulling away from them.

For example, if we choose to stop making negative judgements about other people, this could bother them if making negative judgements about others was something we used to do together. If now we avoid judgemental conversations and stand up for people when they're being judged, our new behaviour can be seen as foreign and uncomfortable.

Community increases happiness

In communities we can all learn together. When we're going through changes we can take the opportunity to share our change with friends. By sharing our journey of change and hearing about how other people are changing and learning is inspiring and motivating.

Meik Wiking is the CEO of the Happiness Institute in Copenhagen. Meik says his job *is to rock up around the world and see what drives happiness, to understand the mechanics of happiness and find ways that people can become happier.*

Meik says, *One of the best predictors of whether people are happy or not, is their relationships. The sense of togetherness, that sense of belonging, that sense of community that impacts people's happiness.*

Part of his research was to sit in cafes all across the world systematically recording how often people smile. Some cities such as London and New York didn't do as well as others, and Meik says, *In London and New York people often walk by themselves.*

Meik says, *If we want to find happiness right now, one of the best ways to do that is to find experiences where we lose sense of ourselves and lose sense of time. It's a pleasant state to be in when we finally shut that little voice in the back of our mind off, and to be fully present in the moment.*

In his book, *The Little Book of Lykke* [Lu-keh] and the Danish word for happiness, he says *It's difficult to measure happiness. Up until now it's been measured by something more tangible – money, and income per capita.* He goes on to say *happiness can mean different things to different people. You may have one perception of what happiness is, I may have another.*

What he cares about in his research is *how you **feel** about **your** life*. That is what counts, and he believes (like we do) that you are the best judge of that.

We can have a happy disposition because different areas of our lives are going well, yet in a given moment when something goes wrong, we may feel sad, angry, frustrated. This does not mean we are not happy. We are just not happy in that moment.

Meik says, *Think of the best possible life you could lead and the worst possible. Where do you stand right now? For you the best possible life imaginable could involve fame and fortune or it might mean staying home to home-school your kids. To me they are equally valid dreams. When trying to evaluate happiness, the important information is what your dream is and how close you feel to living that dream.*

How happy are you right now and how happy are you overall? According to Meik these are two different states we can distinguish to measure happiness. There are ways we can all increase our day-to-day happiness so we can improve the overall quality of our lives.

The World Happiness Report uses six factors to measure the happiness gap: *togetherness or sense of community, money, health, freedom, trust and kindness.*

> *Community gives us a sense of purpose and connection. Happiness can come from knowing we are a part of something bigger than ourselves. It takes us out of our sense of self and gives us greater meaning.*

The Happiness Research Institute found that the happiest countries have a strong sense of community, and the happiest people find they have someone they can rely on in times of need. The Danes are among the people in countries who meet most often with their friends and family and trust that their friends will catch them if they fall. It's no surprise that they are among the world's happiest people.

Ways we can connect and support one another
- Create a weekly or fortnightly ritual coffee shop meet up
- Learn a creative pursuit such as painting
- Attend dance classes
- Join a walking or bushwalking group
- Join a bookclub
- Attend a laughing class
- Go to a comedy night
- Learn something new
- Browse a second hand book shop
- Take a bike ride or join a bike riding club

> *Happiness tip: Make time to eat. Reclaim your lunchtime and sit with friends, family and colleagues, and enjoy eating food slowly and with company.*
>
> – Meik Wiking, *The Little Book of Lykke*

Story – The little town of Nhill

The country town of Nhill in Victoria was shrinking. Many of the townspeople were of the older generation. In 2010 the town warmly welcomed Karen-Burmese refugees from Myanmar. These families were from a minority ethnic group who had suffered trauma and had no country to call home. When they came to Nhill many of them became employed at Luv-a-Duck, a poultry company who had previously found it difficult to find enough workers. Other refugees have obtained work on farms and in other businesses.

The townspeople and the refugees supported each other, had meetups and even swapped recipes. The refugees brought life to the town and boosted its economy.

New friends can come from all cultures, ethnic groups and different social backgrounds. We can learn from one another and see our differences as opportunities to expand our knowledge and experience of the world.

We all get to choose who we want to spend our time with. Our social life isn't meant to be hard – it's meant to bring joy. When we support each other and cheer each other on, life will be easier.

POWER ACTION

Your Friends List

Write a list of the people in your life you spend time with.

Then list:

> Ones you want to spend more time with that lift you up
>
> Send a note, card or text to people you treasure but haven't seen in a while
>
> Are there any you have recently felt a little uncomfortable with. Why? Is there a conversation or another action you need to take that honours you as well as them?
>
> Send a friendly note to a neighbour you don't know or haven't seen in a while
>
> Decide one new person or group you'd like to reach out to in some way

Key Points

- A good friend is one who cheers us on
- A good friend encourages our passions and pursuits
- Through life there can be occasions when we need to rethink our friends
- Having a village around us brings connection
- Having a village brings us belonging and joy
- Take time to treasure the people who enrich our lives

Chapter 13

Coming home

WHERE RESPECT AND EQUALITY IS CULTIVATED

When our home can inspire us to get up every day, to learn something new about the world and learn something new about ourselves, it's a foundation to imagination and freedom.

Our home is a place where we deserve to thrive, not just survive... a place where everyone living there can have frank yet respectful conversations, where the old traditions, beliefs and attitudes about inequality can safely be challenged and evolve into conversations that foster equality.

That can only happen where there is freedom to have courageous conversations. Through these conversations we can test and measure our assumptions and look out at the world and not only see the beauty, but also see the bigger possibilities.

Imagine a home where every woman, man and child has the equal opportunity to live with respect and dignity they deserve. This is a home, that no matter how big or small, no matter what our circumstances, and no matter what location or country – even if we're living in a tent – waters the seeds of possibility. We don't have to have a castle for that to be possible. It all starts with a dream for things to be different.

It's not through material possessions that we grow love, respect and dignity. It's through love itself that we make that possible. Our home is where we can be leaders and role models, where we can imagine a world beyond what is. It's where we can become movers and shakers of the world in some small way, through our radical ideas of equality.

Our home is where others learn that we care enough to give time and space to ourselves. It's a place that fosters our own continual personal growth as much as we foster it in our children. If we are constantly sacrificing ourselves for others in our home to the detriment of our own wellbeing, we risk having our children mirror that behaviour.

On the other hand, a home that is full of acceptance, love and joy, is a home that cultivates growth mindsets. How we all feel when we step inside our environment that matters. This is about us creating an environment we love. One that fosters each person's individual vision. The home we create is part of the legacy we leave.

Our imagination and vision for a better life and a better world happens in a respectful, curious and thriving home.

– Jeanette

When there's no home

It's important to acknowledge that not everyone has a home or a home that feels safe. Domestic violence is a leading cause of homelessness in Australia.

As we write this, 116,427 people in Australia have no home, according to Homelessness Australia.

Based on national reports it was estimated that no less than 150 million people, or about two percent of the world's population were homeless. However, about 1.6 billion, more than 20 percent of the world's population, may lack adequate housing.

– Joseph Chamie, As Cities Grow, So Do the Numbers of Homelessness, Yale University in 2017

Accurately assessing the number of homeless people worldwide is challenging. Definitions of homelessness vary from country to country. Many people are couch surfing. Others are in tents or sleeping rough. Others are staying in severely overcrowded buildings, boarding houses or in temporary accommodation. People who don't have a home to belong in are adversely affected across every area of their lives. It can be almost impossible to have good physical and mental health, let alone work or study.

Many of us have been fortunate enough to have a roof to call home. However, that doesn't guarantee we will feel that we truly belong where we live. Even if we have a home, we're not necessarily going to feel as though we belong in it.

Whatever space we use to call home, the underlying concern for all of us is to have a place in which to belong and to have dignity and respect.

Living with one another

Privacy and space can be a challenge to achieve in families, especially when people who are sharing bedrooms. But there are other ways we can create space and give each other the privacy we yearn for. Sacred spaces can be created around the home and they don't have to be big – just enough for one person to feel as though they have somewhere to retreat to.

Many of us have felt ourselves disappear under the needs of other people. By being very clear about our expectations we can declutter and claim space for ourselves. Equally, it's important to spend time together, to learn about one another and share our concerns and achievements. Home needs to be a place where we learn about the values that are important to us.

Choose values that consider the needs of everyone in the house. Here are some examples of standards and values people may like to include.
- Privacy
- Cleanliness
- Respect
- Teamwork
- Rituals
- Boundaries

Singles or partnerships

No matter what your circumstances, you absolutely deserve to have a home that feels great every time you walk in the front door. Asking for what you need and want is as valid in families as it is for singles and couples, or those living in shared homes. If your only space to retreat to is a bedroom, make sure you've created an environment you are happy to be in on your own... one that feels comfortable and contains the things that bring you joy.

Conversations

What conversations do you need to have to make sure everyone's values are respected? This is about being clear about what's important to you and learning how to express that, then helping other family members do the same. It's about making and managing commitments and promises. When someone breaks their promise, it means being comfortable enough to have the necessary conversations. In this scenario everyone is a learner.

Declutter

How do you feel when you walk into your home? Does it make you smile? Or does it overwhelm you? When we declutter our environment we also declutter our mind from distractions.

Marie Kondo is famous for her book, *Spark Joy*. Her simple concept is to empty everything from an entire wardrobe or from cupboards, drawers, or even an entire room and put it in a pile to be sorted individually. Then begins the sorting. The individual owner of the clothing and items then holds up each item one by one and asks themselves if it brings them joy. If it does, then they keep it. If not, and if it is not useful, it is thanked for its time of service – and given away or sold. Everything kept is valued and has its own place.

> *Minimalism frees the mind from clutter and encourages contentment, clarity of thought and creativity to express ourselves.*
>
> – Laura

Express your unique preferences

Different colours can create different moods. What colours do you like the most? What artwork do you enjoy? Even choosing different cushions or throw rugs can change the mood. Freshening up a space doesn't have to be complicated... it's amazing how a couple of little changes can lift the energy for you.

Hygge has been called everything from 'the art of intimacy', cosiness of the soul' and 'the absence of annoyance' to 'taking pleasure of the presence of gentle, soothing things', 'cosy togetherness' and, my personal favourite, 'cocoa by candlelight.' Hygge is about an atmosphere and an experience, rather than about things. It is about being with the people we love. A feeling of home. A feeling that we are safe, that we are shielded from the world and allow ourselves to let our guard down.

– Meik Wiking, The Little Book of Hygge: The Danish Search for the World's Happiest People

POWER ACTION

What actions do you want to take to create an environment you'll love? And are there any conversations you need to have?

Commit to one small, low or no cost change per week. Have a conversation with your family members and ask them to get on board.

Key Points

- It's important to have a home that reflects how we want to feel
- Decluttering creates a sense of calm
- Have conversations to make sure everyone's values are respected
- Create a space for each person to have for themselves
- For home to be where the heart is, it needs to be a place where respect and equality is cultivated

Chapter 14

Put Yourself First

SELF-CARE THAT FOSTERS YOUR GROWTH

An old outdated belief that has lingered in society is the attitude that women must put others first at their own expense.
Often, this may first become evident when a woman is in a committed relationship or has a child. Much of society has the mentality that putting partners and children first is noble. Obviously we need to nurture our loved ones, however, this is not what we're talking about here. We're talking about putting ourselves last at the expense of our own wellbeing, self-development and sharing our gifts with the world.

The old belief that we have to be everything to everyone corresponds to the outdated story that this noble way of living makes us a good partner or a good mother. It gives us the validation that we are fulfilling that duty, but many times at the expense of our own dreams and desires.

Many women reach the age of 50+ and wonder what they've done with their lives. They become frightened that they don't have current skills and lack the financial freedom to make choices. They worry about their future and fear getting older.

The sooner we start putting ourselves first, the sooner we can be the leader we were always born to be. This means sharing our gifts and role modeling these practices to our children, nieces and nephews. Children need to see us as leaders in action, so they can grow up and be leaders in their own lives.

Many women in the workforce work really hard for others but they don't often value their own skills and talents. We often haven't put our hands up for promotions because to do so would be to go against everything we've learned about being humble and putting ourselves last. It would disrupt the status quo if we stepped outside our own comfort zone, took a risk and showed up as confident. So we play small.

Putting ourselves first doesn't mean we have to stop doing things for others, especially if this brings us joy. However, it does mean re-evaluating where we put ourselves last at the expense of our own happiness and future opportunities.

There is power in putting ourselves first. The more we value ourselves, the more will get to know ourselves and expand our opportunities. The more opportunities we create, the more possibilities we will start to see.

Traditionally, women carry the invisible mental and emotional load for everyone else. They often survive on limited sleep. The payoff? That we're seeing others content. When we try to do it all, something has to give... and it's usually us. And it shouldn't be.

Many of us have felt as if we have disappeared. In the quest to look after others, it's very easy to lose ourselves. When mothers decide they want to go back to work, run a business or learn a new skill, they can be burdened with an awful lot of guilt. This is because they are trying so hard to juggle everything, and without realising it, placing their worth on the ability to fulfill several roles. This is a mountainous standard with a recipe for burnout and dissatisfaction. It may be necessary to to loosen up our standards so they don't impact our health and wellbeing.

We are enough without striving for perfection in every area of our lives. For example, writing this book means Laura's lawn is beginning to look like a hairy jungle and Jeanette's house has dog hair all over the floors and furniture.

Putting ourselves first can feel very isolating when our identity and self-worth is tied up in all the things we provide for other people. When we reach that life phase when everyone we have cared for is beginning to move on, we can be left with grief and sadness and feel like we're no longer needed.

Putting ourselves first may be something very new. It's important for our children to see what self-care looks like. Children don't learn from us telling them what to do, they learn from us showing them.

Story – Putting myself last

I put others before myself most of my life. I didn't know who I was but I spent a lot of time getting to know who other people were and what they needed. I was the go-to person. I supported others when they were faced with challenges. I heard that sometimes you need to put yourself last so that others can get what they need. I had no idea what I needed or wanted because I'd never stopped to figure it out.

When my children left home I felt relief and sadness all at once, and it took me years to find who I was. I went to my first coaching conference feeling nervous and worried that I wouldn't fit in. I was concerned that I might talk to someone who would see me as a fraud. This was the result of believing I wasn't enough. Years of people pleasing and being everything to everyone else took over my being. At one conference while we were working on what we were feeling in our bodies, I declared I couldn't really feel my body. Then I said, *I don't have a body below the neck*. The only way I could describe it was that I'd shut myself off. Interestingly, it took months of practice after that day to start feeling again. I had to give myself permission to set aside time to do my daily practices and write my reflections on the papers we were assigned. By signing up to the course I had made a choice. I had to come first, and learning about this incredible phenomenon was the most liberating time I've ever had.

I encourage you that no matter what age you are and no matter what your circumstances are or what life phase you are in, start now.

– Jeanette

Here's some things we can do put ourselves first...

1. Meditation or prayer

Meditation or prayer calms down our nervous system (the fight or flight mechanism). It's incredibly good for the body, reducing blood pressure and heart rate and boosting the immune system. It helps to reset your nervous system.

It gives us powerful abilities to step outside the chaos and stresses of the world. It's the epitome of responding to the world instead of reacting to it.

Meditation is something we can practice and get better at over time.

FACT: In his TED-ED video 'How Stress Affects Your Brain', Madhumita Murgia states that meditation is key in reversing the damage cortisol has had on our brains. He says that meditation involves breathing deeply and being aware and focused on our surroundings.

Through meditation we can visualise a future we want to have.

Even just a few minutes a day can bring us some calm and inner peace. We can meditate almost anywhere. Breathe slowly and deeply to allow maximum refreshing oxygen. Allow your thoughts to wander and then bring them back gently to the meditation.

There are meditation apps that can teach and guide us through meditation.

Some different types of meditation:
- **Prayer** – talking to a higher power, such as God, the universe
- **Guided Meditation** – listening to a spoken meditation
- **Gratitude Meditation** – focussing on feelings of gratitude, love, kindness
- **Mindfulness Meditation** – being mindful of your environment
- **Mantra Meditation** – the repetition of a calming word or a sentence
- **Yoga** – various poses and steady breathing
- **Tai Chi Meditation** – a Chinese martial art technique
- **Qigong Meditation** – a combination of movement, breathing

2. Get moving

FACT: Exercise reduces our levels of adrenaline and cortisol – stress hormones. It helps us produce endorphins in our brain to help us feel good and even reduces pain. It helps enhance our body's ability to heal itself, boosts our immunity and helps us feel great.

We tend to think of exercise as a preventative measure – something that helps us maintain our general fitness and keep excess weight at bay. But in reality, exercise has a vast range of healing influences on the body – influences that can help reverse negative biochemical trends, while improving our resiliency and immunity at virtually every level of our physiology.

– Susan Gaines, How Exercise Heals, experiencelife.com

Exercise is a mood manoeuvre – yes, it shifts our moods. As we exercise, our nervous system settles, and we begin to shift into more elevated emotional states. This gives us the ability to think more clearly and make better decisions. We can include exercise in our day in bursts of a few minutes. A 30-minute walk four to five days a week consistently will make a huge impact on our health.

3. Nutrition

Just like a car without fuel, our body and mind will be struggling to function at its best if we don't give ourselves the nutrients and vitamins needed. Good nutrition boosts our immunity, helps to combat daily stress and boosts our mood.

Nutritionist Kimberley Douglas highly recommends cutting sugar and smoking and reducing caffeine. She also recommends looking at how hormone levels, gluten, dairy and insufficient protein may be affecting us – as **every** body is different.

This is not about being confused by all the 'perfect diets' on the market. This is about listening to **your** body and asking it what's missing and what it needs right now. Our body is our intuitive guide. There are lots of low cost options to getting enough nutrition in our diet.

Food is about pleasure as well as health. If we're going to have a chocolate, we should enjoy it. Guilt causes stress to the body. It's not healthy or helpful to judge ourselves for eating what society says we **shouldn't** eat.

4. Indulge

Do what nurtures you. And. Take. Your. Time. Treat yourself with value. This is an essential part of the process of long term health and it also creates the habit of a long term healthy physical and mental lifestyle.

It'd be great to go to a tropical island for a couple of weeks... but let's get real, many of us are not going to have that opportunity at our fingertips when we need it. In the meantime, we can indulge ourselves in all kinds of ways, without spending much money.

While it's lovely to be around friends, spend some time in your own company too. Get to know more of what makes you, you.

Some ideas:
- Stroll through parklands
- Watch a movie with your favourite treats
- Hang with a friend who makes you laugh
- Have a long soak in the bath with Epsom salts
- Have a cup of tea, some chocolate and read a favourite book
- Do your nails, have a massage
- Take yourself out for breakfast, lunch or dinner
- Buy yourself a little something that brings you joy

5. Get adventurous

Try new things! Experiencing and learning things prompts our brains to create brand new neural pathways. Doing things we haven't done before (or that we haven't done in many years) also proves that the world is there for us to explore.

> A few ideas:
> - Rock climb
> - Ski or snowboard
> - Hot air ballooning
> - Rollerblading
> - Horse riding
> - Paragliding
> - Painting
> - See a live show
> - Go to Meetups
> - Try different cultural cuisines
> - Volunteer at a soup kitchen
> - Visit a refugee centre

6. Creativity

Be creative with a pen or pencil in your hand. Let the ink flow without thinking.

Write about the you that you want to be. Write about the life you want to have, about the places you'd like to travel to, and the sorts of people you'd like to meet. Write about what your dream day could look like.

Create your own vision board. This can be as simple as sticking images and words onto cardboard that represent what you'd love to have in your life ahead. Write about or take photos of some little things that bring you joy. The smell of rain? The taste of a strawberry? A flower opening? A bird taking flight? By focusing on the little things that bring you joy, you will attract more of them **and** invite a mood of gratitude. It's a universal law.

Putting ourselves first is as much a practice as it is a way of being

To do it we have to first make it a priority. Then from a priority, create a practice, and from a practice, create a habit. The only person who can make this decision for us, is us. This means valuing ourselves so much that we will do for ourselves what we've done for everyone else. We may have moved heaven and earth for other people. Now it's our turn.

This is not about putting ourselves under pressure, but thinking of self-care as fun and playing around with different ideas. The more we give ourselves self-care, the stronger and more independent we will become because it is coming from our own inner strength, rather than seeking it outside of ourselves.

POWER ACTION

Create New Habits

Putting ourselves first feels unfamiliar to many of us, especially if we've been the go-to woman for much of our lives. Inequality has shaped the way we take care of others. Often that means putting others first. Creating new habits means changing old habits, but we have to start with a new habit first, then do it over and over again.

Pick one new habit you would like to form. It could be to add one or two extra days of exercise into your routine, or meditating at least a couple of days a week. It could be writing each morning – whatever feels like a nice practice to add into your day.

Stick a note up to remind yourself about it. Also write down what reward you can give yourself after you have succeeded at keeping the new habit for a week.

Key Points

- Meditation and exercise de-stresses us and makes us feel great
- Nutritious food gives us the fuel we need for maximum energy
- Indulge without guilt
- Be adventurous and explore
- Unleash our creativity

Chapter 15

Reflecting Forward
A VISION FOR THE FUTURE

Learning about Good Girl Syndrome is a powerful way of turning our pain into purpose without attaching our stories of the past to our actions of the future. It is about developing new beliefs and practices. It's also about asking for what we want and need, and knowing we have a right to seek the things that bring us joy and freedom to choose.

In the Age of Information we can access and learn about anything we want. We can search the internet to make choices about our health and wellbeing. We can learn online, offline and on social media which has given us the power to step outside of our own limitations and make choices we've never made before. Through the power of learning we can find things that bring us meaning and give us purpose.

Even though we have access to copious amounts of information, none of that is worthwhile if we leave ourselves behind in the process.

Putting ourselves first gives us the space to think, and the time to reflect, learn and create new opportunities. We can use our creativity by finding new creative ventures and we can explore anything that we're interested in.

It's important to believe anything is possible, rather than being stuck in the Resignation Trap, wishing our life was different. There's power in imagining our ideal life, and there's also value in taking steps straight away. Every step we take toward the future we want will be a step closer to what we want.

We encourage you to take powerful actions, to be the change you want to see for yourself and in the world. Changing you from the inside out means changing what is no longer serving you. It means improving your interactions and having better relationships. It also means using your power for good by making a difference in the world.

Neither of us, Jeanette and Laura, believed enough in ourselves and both of us were living with Good Girl Syndrome without realising it, but we had one thing in common – the drive and determination to make a difference in the world. We've both been on huge learning curves. None of this would be possible without the hundreds of conversations, personal learning and reflections about what we wanted this book to be. As time went on we saw more and more possibilities.

We invite you to use this time in your life to learn about yourself and move away from the outdated narratives such as Good Girl and 'being everything to everyone'.

You don't have to be the Good Girl but you can learn from your Good Girl experiences to help you do whatever the heck you want. You do not ever have to wait for anyone else to give you that authority. Your authority is there waiting for you, you just have to take it and don't let anyone or anything stop you.

Here are some practices that will enhance your ability to visualise a positive future:

- Be in service not in sacrifice
- Only make promises when they don't equal sacrifice
- Ask for what you want and need
- Stop making promises that equal sacrifice
- Create daily rituals
- Practice gratitude
- Be a learner of your moods and emotions
- Shift into resourceful moods
- See future self as uplifting, strong, capable
- Go out and have new conversations with people
- Say no when yes wouldn't serve you
- Have difficult conversations
- Ask for a pay rise
- Do some action research around the things you are good at and love doing
- Search and apply for new jobs
- Explore possible business ideas
- Create a vision board

- Listen to meditation
- Join Meetup groups
- Start your own Meetup group
- Enrol in courses that help you new life practices become a reality

Nothing is stopping us from changing our reality except if we're still living from our past reality. The invisible gender, cultural and social narratives and practices we've lived in are outdated. They no longer need to infuse themselves into our homes and our professional lives. There are opportunities and possibilities everywhere. All we need to do is allow them in one day at a time.

Finally – make a promise to yourself that will create the change you want to see in your life. Your promise might sound something like this...

I promise I will look toward the future and see all the possibilities that are available to me.

Most of all, have fun with your life. You are your greatest teacher, your only true authority and your biggest cheerleader.

About the Authors

Together we are Power in Your Pocket

For free resources and tips, plus courses to rebel from a life of **shoulds**, see us at:

WEBSITE: www.powerinyourpocket.com.au
EMAIL: powerinyourpocket.info@gmail.com
FACEBOOK: www.facebook.com/powerinyourpocket
INSTAGRAM: @power_in_your_pocket

Jeanette

Jeanette is an expert in personal development. In co-authoring her first book *Power in Your Pocket: Detox from Good Girl Syndrome*, she has become a game changer in eradicating the doubt that women experience, world wide. She is an inspirational speaker, Ontological Coach, Trainer and Workshop Facilitator. Jeanette's clients say she is, powerfully connected, in tuned, insightful and has the ability to zero in on their deepest concerns and challenges so that true transformation is possible.

She has a passion for supporting women step uninhibited into the next phase of life, find their voice so they can live confidently as the leader they were born to be. Having a background in small business, her superpower is transforming women to develop a deep intuition, lead themselves first, then lead others from the heart. Jeanette runs one-on-one coaching programs, transformational and personal leadership workshops.

Jeanette loves to hang out with her adult children and grandchildren. She loves anything to do with sunsets, beach and travel. She loves working from her local beach close to her home in a suburb of Brisbane.

If you want someone who truly connects, listens deeply and powerfully leads her audience toward self-transformation, you can reach Jeanette here:

WEBSITE: www.jeanettemundy.com
FACEBOOK: www.facebook.com/jeanettemundy
INSTAGRAM: @jeanette_mundy

Laura

Laura is a freelance copywriter for non-for-profits and businesses making the world a better place. She combines her creative background with intuitive writing to tap into the emotions and needs of an audience and get results.

As a co-author of *Power In Your Pocket: Detox From Good Girl Syndrome* this book shares her learning and research in discovering her own inner rebel from a life of 'shoulds'. It is her mission to help women and girls worldwide to see that they can empower themselves to create a future free of control from others – or any limitations. Her dream is that each woman, man, boy and girl work together for a world where equality and respect is a given.

Laura loves to spend pockets of her time drinking chai tea, writing her tween novel, drawing and photography, exploring nature and hanging with family and friends in the leafy area of Greensborough, Melbourne, Australia.

If you need a caring, professional writer for your non-for-profit or change-maker business, you can reach Laura here:

WEBSITE: www.lauralehare.com
FACEBOOK: www.tinyurl.com/FacebookLauraLeLievre
INSTAGRAM: @lauralehare

Reference List

Anatomy of the Spirit, The Seven Stages of Power and Healing. Myss, Caroline C. (1997). Australia. Random House Australia.

Big Workshop Manual for Coaching and Leadership In Action (workbook). Sieler, Alan.

'Bridget Jones Bridget Jones' Baby' (Movie). Renee Zellweger, (2016) *Coaching to the Human Soul Ontological Coaching and Deep Change Volume II.* Sieler, Alan. (2007). Publishing Solutions.

Daring Greatly, How the Courage to be Vulnerable Transforms How We Live, Love, Parent and Lead. Brown, Brene. (2012). USA. Penguin Books, Ltd.

Delusions of Gender: How Our Minds, Society and Neurosexism Create Difference. Fine, Cordelia. (2010). USA. W. W. Norton and Company.

Fight Like a Girl. Ford, Clementine. (2016). Allen and Unwin.

Goodnight Stories for Rebel Girls: 100 Tales of Extraordinary Women. Favilli, Elena and Cavallo Francesca. (2017). Great Britain. Particular Books.

How to Raise Confident Girls (PDF). Favilli, Elena. (2016). Timbuktu Labs.

Managing Stress: Principles and Strategies for Health and Wellbeing. Seaward, Brian. (2006). London. Jones and Bartlett Learning.

Rising Strong, How the Ability to Reset Transforms the Way We Live, Love, Parent, and Lead. Brown, Brené. (2017). Random House.

Spark Joy. Kondo, Marie. (2017). Ebury Publishing.

The Confidence Code: The Science and Art of Self-Assurance – What Women Should Know. Shipman, Claire and Kay, Katty. (2016). HarperCollins Publishers Inc.

The Curse of the Good Girl: Raising Authentic Girls with Courage and Confidence. Simmons, Rachel. (2009). Penguin Books.

The Gifts of Imperfection, Let go of Who You Think You're Supposed to Be and Embrace Who You Are. Brown, Brene. (2010). Hazelden Publishing.

The Little Book of Hygge: The Danish Search for the Worlds Happiest People. Wiking, Meiki. (2017). Penguin Life.

The Motivation Manifesto: Declarations to Claim Your Personal Power. Burchard, Brendon. (2014). Hay House Inc.

The Organized Mind: Thinking Straight in the Age of Information Overload. Levitin, David. (2015). Penguin Books Ltd.

The Power of Hope. Karapanagiotidis, Kon. (2018). HarperCollins Publishers (Australia) Pty Limited.

The Unopened Gift, A Primer in Emotional Literacy. Newby, Dan and Lunz, Lucy. (2017). Daniel Newby.

Where Has My Little Girl Gone? Carey, Tanith. (2011). A Lion Book (England).

Why Does He Do That? In the Minds of Angry and Controlling Men. Bancroft, Lundy. (2002). Penguin Group.

Who Switched Off My Brain? Controlling Toxic Thoughts and Emotions. Leaf, Caroline. (2009). Thomas Nelson Inc.

You Can Heal Your Life. Hay, Louise. (1984). Hay House Inc.

WEB

ABC Earshot. 'Marriage Bar Abolished, Marriage in Australia: A Timeline of How Love and Law Have Changed in 130 Years.' Gollan, Kathy. (Updated 23 May 2018).
https://www.abc.net.au/news/2017-04-17/ marriage-in-australia-how-love-and-law-have-changed-in-130-years/8430254

ABC Life. 'How to even up housework with your partner.' Jennings-Edquist, Grace. (Updated 28 August 2019). *www.abc.net.au/life/how-to-even-up-housework-with-your-partner/11289272*

ABC Life. 'What do you do when you're sick of carrying the mental load for your household?' Updated 23rd October 2019). *www.abc.net.au/life/when-youre-sick-of-carrying-the-mental-load-for-your-household/11292628*

ABC Life. 'Why is it So Hard For Men to Link Their Personal Behaviour to Gender Inequality?' Osman Faruqi, Osman. (Updated 13 August 2019). *www.abc.net.au/life/why-men-struggle-to-link-behaviour-to-gender-equality/11314468*

ABC News – The Conversation. 'Women Aren't Better Multitaskers Than Men – They're Just Doing More Work. Ruppanner, Leah. (15 Aug 2019). *www.abc.net.au/news/2019-08-15/multitasking-women-and-men/11414540*

ABC. Q&A (YouTube). 'Women in Power and Weaponised Fake News.' Hilary, Clinton and Gillard, Julia. (10th May 2018) *youtu.be/M-8dICGguOs*

Aletia. 'Why Women Compare Themselves to Each Other.' Bello, Adriana. (Feb 2018) *https://aleteia.org/2018/02/19/why-women-always-compare-themselves-to-each-other*

Australian Bureau of Statistics. 'Work and Family Balance, 4125.0 - Gender Indicators, Australia.' (Feb 2016) *www.abs.gov.au/ausstats/abs@.nsf/Lookup/by%20Subject/4125.0~Feb%202016~Main%20Features~Work%20and%20Family%20Balance~3411*

Australian Women's History Network. 'Rape in Marriage: Why Was it So Hard to Criminalise Sexual Violence?' Featherstone, Lisa. (7th December 2016). *www.auswhn.org.au/blog/marital-rape*

BBC News, '10 Reasons Why Men Opposed Votes For Women, Women's Suffrage'. Gillett, Francesca (2018) *www.bbc.com/news/uk-43740033*

CHIPS Magazine. 'About Grace Hopper'. (Updated March 2017) *www.doncio.navy.mil/chips/ArticleDetails.aspx?ID=2265*

CHIPS Magazine. 'Only the Limits of Our Imagination – Exclusive interview with Rear Adm, Hopper, Grace from Chips Ahoy in 1986.' (April-June 2002) *www.doncio.navy.mil/chips/ArticleDetails.aspx?id=3563*

Elite Daily. 'Why Women Are So Hard On Themselves And Men Don't Think Twice.' Martin, Lauren. (6th November 2015). *www.elitedaily.com/women/women-men-hard-on-yourself-difference/1270534*

Entertainment Weekly. 'Stars Raise Sexual Assault Awareness With #MeToo Twitter Campaign.' Glicksman, Josh. (16th October, 2017). *www.ew.com/news/2017/10/16/me-too-twitter-campaign-alyssa-milano-sexual-assault-awareness/*

Equal Rights Alliance. 'Gender Equality in Australia' (webpage). (27th August 2019) *www.equalityrightsalliance.org.au/who-we-are/gender-equality-in-australia*

Experience Life. 'How Exercise Heals'. Gaines, Susan. (November 2007) *https://experiencelife.com/article/how-exercise-heals*

Exploring Your Mind. '7 Characteristics of Authoritarian People, According to Psychology.' (25th February 25, 2018) *www.exploringyourmind.com/7-characteristics-authoritarian-people*

Fearless Soul. 'Learn How to Control Your Mind, Use this to Brainwash Yourself' (video). Dispenza, Dr Joe. *www.iamfearlesssoul.com/joe-dispenza-you-are-the-creator-of-your-world*

Fortune. '13% of Americans Think Women Are Less "Emotionally Suited" to Politics Than Men.'Bellstrom, Kristen. (16th April 2019). *www.fortune.com/2019/04/16/women-politics-emotions*

Greater Good Magazine. 'How Gratitude Can Help You Through Hard Times.' Emmons, Robert, Ph.D. (13th May, 2013). *www.greatergood.berkeley.edu/profile/robert_emmons*

Greater Good Magazine. 'How Gratitude Changes Your Brain.' Wong, Joel, Ph.D. and Brown, Joshua, Ph.D. (6th June, 2017). *www.greatergood.berkeley.edu/article/item/how_gratitude_changes_you_and_your_brain*

HelpGuide. *www.helpguide.org/about-us.htm*

Homelessness Australia. *www.homelessnessaustralia.org.au/about/homelessness-statistics*

'How Stress Affects Your Brain' (video). Madhumita, Murgia. TEDEd YouTube video (9th November, 2015) *www.youtube.com/watch?v=WuyPuH9ojCE*

HuffPost. 'I am Woman, Hear Me Apologise: My Quest to Stop Saying Sorry all the Damn Time.' Beveridge, Sydney. (26 April, 2018). *www.huffpost.com/entry/women-stop-apologizing_n_5ae0b420e4b04aa23f1e7f09*

Independent, Girls Lose Risk-taking Confidence By the TIme They Reach Adulthood While Male Confidence Grows, Study Shows.' Based on University of Stockholm study. Rachael Pells, (20 August, 2017) *www.independent.co.uk/news/education/education-news/girls-boys-risk-taking-confidence-adulthood-jeopardy-junior-university-stockholm-a7903346.html*

Me Too Movement (website). www.metoomvmt.org/about Our Watch. www.ourwatch.org.au

Psychology Today. '9 Ways to Ease Overwhelm.' Carter, Christine L., Ph.D. (Sep 28, 2016).*www.psychologytoday.com/us/blog/raising-happiness/201609/9-ways-ease-overwhelm*

Quarterly Essay. 'Men at Work, Australia's Parenthood Trap.' Issue 75 2019. Crabb, Annabel. *www.quarterlyessay.com.au/essay/2019/09/men-at-work/extract*

Risk of Homelessness in Older Women. Australian Human Rights Commission. (4th April 2019). *www.humanrights.gov.au/our-work/age-discrimination/projects/risk-homelessness-older-women*

Shame On Shanty. 'The Battlefield of Comparison.' Bleakley, Jennifer. *www.shameonshanty.com/the-battlefield-of-comparison*

Shift. 'Gender Equality.' *www.shiftproject.org/sdgs/gender-equality*

Smart Company. 'Overcoming Defeat, and Why We Need More Women at the Table.' Keating, Eloise. (1st June 2018) *www.smartcompany.com.au*

TED. 'How Childhood Trauma Affects Health Across a Lifetime' (video). Burke, Nadine. *https://www.ted.com/talks/nadine_burke_harris_how_childhood_trauma_affects_health_across_a_lifetime/discussion*

TED Talks India: Nayi Baat. 'Seven Beliefs that Can Silence Women – And How to Unlearn Them' (video). Narayan, Deepa. (May, 2019). *https://www.ted.com/talks/deepa_narayan_7_beliefs_that_can_silence_women_and_how_to_unlearn_them?language=en*

TED Talk Tedwomen. ' Me Too is a Movement, Not a Moment' (video). Burke, Tarana (November 2018) *www.ted.com/talks/tarana_burke_me_too_is_a_movement_not_a_moment?language=en*

TEDxNorrkoping. 'The Power of Believing That You Can Improve, The Power of Yet' (video). (November 2014). Dweck, Carol. *www.ted.com/talks/carol_dweck_the_power_of_believing_that_you_can_improve?language=en*

TEDx RoyalTunbridgeWells. 'How My Gut Changed Everything' (video). Hirst, Rebecca. (2018). *www.tedxroyaltunbridgewells.com/video-blog/2018/how-listening-to-my-gut-changed-everything*

The Atlantic, The Confidence Gap. Kay, Katty and Shipman, Claire. (May 2014 Issue)
www.theatlantic.com/magazine/archive/2014/05/the-confidence-gap/359815

The Call to Courage (Netflix video), Brown, Brene. (April 2019). *www.netflix.com/title/81010166*

The Dictionary of Obscure Sorrows, https://www.dictionaryofobscuresorrows.com/post/23536922667/sonder

The Domestic Violence Resource Centre. www.dvrcv.org.au

The Guardian. 'Male and Female Ability Differences Down to Socialisation, Not Genetics.' (August 14th 2010) *www.theguardian.com/world/2010/aug/15/girls-boys-think-same-way*

The New York Times. 'The Woman Who Created #MeToo Long Before Hashtags.' Garcia, Sandra. (2017). *www.nytimes.com/2017/10/20/us/me-too-movement-tarana-burke.html*

The School of Visibility. 'The Courage to Upset Another.' *www.theschoolofvisibility.com/upsetting-another*

Women's Agenda. 'How to Break Free From the Good Girl Syndrome.' Heading, Jess. (September 20, 2017) *www.womensagenda.com.au/uncategorised/how-to-break-free-from-the-good-girl-syndrome*

World Economic Forum. 'The Global Gender Gap Report 2018' (PDF). *www3.weforum.org/docs/WEF_GGGR_2018.pdf*

The School of Visibility. 'The Courage to Upset Another.' *www.theschoolofvisibility.com/upsetting-another*

The Sydney Morning Herald. 'Transcript of Julia Gillard's Speech About Misogyny.' (October 10, 2012). *www.smh.com.au/politics/federal/transcript-of-julia-gillards-speech-20121010-27c36.html*

The World Health Organisation (WHO) *www.who.int/news-room/fact-sheets/detail/violence-against-women*

The University of Copenhagen. 'Women are Beautiful, Men Rational.' (27th August 2019). *www.news.ku.dk/all_news/2019/08/women-are-beautiful-men-rational*

United Nations. 'Chapter 6, Violence Against Women.' *(2015) www.unstats.un.org/unsd/gender/downloads/WorldsWomen2015_chapter6_t.pdf*

UN WOMEN. *www.unwomen.org*

Women For One. '10 Quotes that will Inspire You to Share Your Story.' (February 18 2015). *www.omenforone.com/10-quotes-to-inspire-you-to-share-your-story*

Yale Global Online, Yale University. 'As Cities Grow, So Do the Numbers of Homelessness'. Chamie, Joseph (July 13 2017), *www.yaleglobal.yale.edu/content/cities-grow-so-do-numbers-homeless*

www.ingramcontent.com/pod-product-compliance
Lightning Source LLC
Chambersburg PA
CBHW042139160426
43201CB00021B/2344